# THE GET ORGANIZED

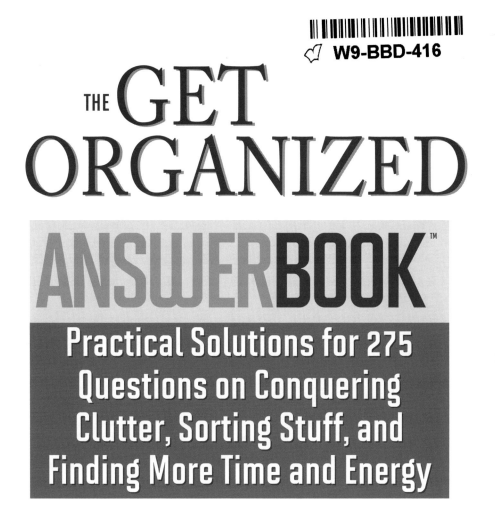

## ANSWER BOOK™

### Practical Solutions for 275 Questions on Conquering Clutter, Sorting Stuff, and Finding More Time and Energy

— JAMIE NOVAK —

SOURCEBOOKS, INC.®
NAPERVILLE, ILLINOIS

Published by Sourcebooks, Inc.
P.O. Box 4410, Naperville, Illinois 60567-4410
(630) 961-3900
Fax: (630) 961-2168
www.sourcebooks.com

Library of Congress Cataloging-in-Publication Data

Novak, Jamie.
  The get organized answer book : practical solutions for 275 questions on conquering clutter, sorting stuff, and finding more time and energy / by Jamie Novak.
      p. cm.
  Includes index.
  1. Storage in the home. 2. Orderliness. 3. Time management. I. Title.
  TX309.N685 2009
  648'.8—dc22
                                    2008038832

Printed and bound in the United States of America.
CHG 10 9 8 7 6 5 4 3 2

# THE GET ORGANIZED

# ANSWERBOOK™

## Practical Solutions for 275 Questions on Conquering Clutter, Sorting Stuff, and Finding More Time and Energy

# Dedication

*This book is dedicated to all of us who strive to live a life we love, because we know this is not a dress rehearsal. It may not be easy, but we strive to get organized and save time so we can reach for our dreams and enjoy the important things in life. Sure, some days we're more successful than others. Yet we get up each day with a renewed sense of hope that we can overcome the overwhelming and live a life we love by tackling each day in bite-size pieces.*

# Contents

# *Acknowledgments*

First and foremost I want to express my appreciation to all of the not-so-organized people who have shared their challenges about getting and staying organized. Without your honesty this book would not be possible. I'm grateful to be a part of your quest to create a life you love by getting organized and saving time.

To my literary agent, Jessica Faust, I am honored to be working with you. Your guidance and advice continue to prove invaluable. Many thanks to the entire team at Sourcebooks, including my fantastic editor Shana Drehs, my hardworking publicists Heather Moore and Emily Mullen, and the gifted editor of this book, Sara Appino.

I extend my thanks to my family, and most especially Erik, Kiara, and William, who not only bring laughter and joy to my life but also provide me with ample writing material. Lastly to my good friends, most notably, Tom and Lee Aljian and John and Lee Coffey. Your ideas inspire me and your support means the world to me.

# Introduction

I'm guessing you have some questions about how to get organized in one or more areas of your life. Whether you're fairly organized and looking for a few more tips, you're completely disorganized and don't know where to start, or you're somewhere in between, I promise you'll find answers in this book.

The great news is that the answers I've compiled are solutions that I use, so they're tried and true. *The Get Organized Answer Book* offers in-depth answers to a wide range of the most frequently asked questions on organizing, and it complements my book of quick tips on the subject, *1,000 Quick and Easy Organizing Solutions*. *The Get Organized Answer Book* will be your go-to book for organization solutions for all areas of your life for years to come.

As I travel the country presenting my programs on Bite-Size Organizing, I fill journals with the questions posed to me during the Q&A part of the program. I used these notes to help create the questions and answers in this book. I wrote this book with you in mind. I made sure to give concise, realistic, and content-rich answers to ensure you get the most from this book.

I know that organizing can feel overwhelming, especially if you've put it off for some time. You might feel hopeless, especially when other people you know seem to be naturally organized. Trying to stay on top of things every day can take every bit of energy you have, but I promise that when you use the solutions provided in this book, you'll feel more successful, in control, energized, and free. You want that, don't you? I wrote this book to help you achieve that feeling. We're a team now—you can lean on me for support as you take bite-size steps toward creating a life you love!

## How to Use This Book

I wrote this book in an easy-to-digest format so you can carry it around and find solutions quickly. Although you can read the book cover to cover, chances are that if you wait until you have the time to do that, you'll never start. Instead, read a little here and a little there, internalizing one or two answers at a time. You'll see that each chapter contains questions on a similar topic, like your kitchen, office, or green ideas. Each question is followed by a concise yet complete answer, packed with helpful suggestions that allow you to take action right away.

No matter how you start reading this book, at least you've started. After all, taking action is the first step to getting more organized. It is that easy: just read and do, then read some more and do some more. I know you're busy so I've taken great care to create realistic solutions that will help you organize your life in no time. Let's not waste another minute. Turn to chapter 1 or skim the table of contents for your topic of interest, and start reading. I encourage you to read at least one question now—the answer to that question might help you build the momentum to start organizing.

As you read the questions and answers in this book, keep in mind that whenever an answer suggests tossing something, that doesn't mean the only option is to literally toss the item into the garbage. You can toss it into a recycling bin, or toss it into a bag to give to charity or to a friend. I've included many resources for ways to share your stuff. Now you're ready to turn the page and start organizing.

# Chapter 1

# BEHIND THE SCENES Q&A

- What is clutter?
- Where does clutter come from?
- How much time can a person lose every day due to disorganization?
- How do I know if my clutter is normal?
- How do I know if I would be classified as a compulsive hoarder?
- Can clutter be a safety concern?
- Is it true that having perfectionist tendencies can actually lead to disorganization?
- Free items or sale items aren't really clutter, are they?
- Did I inherit my disorganization?
- I used to be super-organized; now I can't even find my keys. What happened?
- What's the best test for assessing how organized I am?
- When will I finally be organized?
- What are the root causes of disorganization?
- Can clutter affect my well-being?
- Can clutter affect my body weight?
- I feel isolated and lonely; could that be due to the clutter?
- Can my attitude affect my ability to organize?
- I simply lack the energy to get started. How can I get motivated?
- Why am I so organized at work but not at home?
- I seem to sabotage myself when trying to get organized. Why?
- Could the fact that I'm easily distracted be caused by clutter?
- My home is so cluttered that I don't like being there. What can I do?
- Is it possible to save money by getting organized?
- Is disorganization simply a bad habit?
- Are horizontal surfaces a bad idea?
- Can furniture choices affect my level of organization?

- How long will it take me to get organized?
- Is a home truly a reflection of the person who lives there?
- How can I ensure success or at least better my odds of getting organized?
- Is there any way to avoid feeling defeated at the end of the day?
- How can I stop losing things the minute I put them down?
- Will increasing my memory help me get organized?
- Why do I have conversations or internal debates with myself?
- Why does clutter make me feel so guilty?
- Does clutter affect my mood?
- Why do I feel like I need permission to let go of things?
- I always second-guess myself and talk myself into keeping things. What can I do?

## What is clutter?

My definition of clutter is any item that falls into one or more of three categories:

1. Things you do not use or love (three extra spatulas in the kitchen utensil drawer)
2. Things without a home (the new shirt you just bought that is draped over the back of a chair because your dresser is overstuffed)
3. Anything unfinished or in need of repair (the sweater sitting on the washing machine that is missing a button)

## Where does clutter come from?

Sometimes it seems like clutter falls from the sky; as quickly as you clear one area, it gets cluttered again. I've noticed that each person accumulates clutter in a different way. Which of the following describes you?

- Holding on to an item thinking it might come in handy one day
- Putting an item down and planning to deal with it later
- Being unwilling to let something go simply because it's still good
- Getting stuck in a perfectionist rut and waiting to do the organizing project perfectly
- Having a sentimental attachment to items because they remind you of something
- Taking items home just because they are on sale or free

One or more of these accumulation methods can create clutter. Knowing how you create clutter can help you to deal with it.

## How much time can a person lose every day due to disorganization?

On average a person wastes ninety minutes a day looking for lost or misplaced things. This might sound like an unbelievable amount of time, but when you stop to think about it, you might find that the time you waste is average or above average depending on the day. Think of it like this: Add up five minutes spent searching for car keys, plus ten minutes lost waiting for a child to locate a backpack, plus fifteen minutes wasted waiting for take-out dinner since you forgot to defrost something to cook. See how quickly you can lose a half hour? That doesn't take into account time you might waste looking through emails in your inbox, searching for a scrap of paper with a phone number written on it, or running extra errands. Imagine what you can do with that wasted time. Gaining extra minutes can be great motivation for getting organized.

## How do I know if my clutter is normal?

The general rule is that if clutter is not affecting your day-to-day living, then you're doing all right. Like most rules, however, this one has exceptions. Some people are unable or unwilling to recognize that clutter is disrupting their lives. Here are the top ten signs of an overly cluttered life:

1. Unexpected guests send you into "scoop and dump" mode. That means before you can answer the door, you grab a bag or laundry basket and frantically scoop up piles of paper, toys, clothes, etc., dumping them in a closet, bedroom, or garage. Once your guests leave, you don't address the clutter you just moved.

2. You misplace things on a daily basis. Everyday accessories like a cell phone, keys, pen, purse, shoes, jacket—you get the picture.

3. You live out of a laundry basket. Clothes are washed and folded, yet there is no space in the closet or dresser drawers to hang them up or put them away.

4. Piles of "important" papers are stacked on surfaces (and possibly the floor) throughout your home. You leave them out as a visual reminder so you won't forget to act on them.

5. You stash stuff in one or more areas of your home, planning to decide what to do with it later. But later never comes. You might use the garage, basement, attic, spare/guest bedroom, or other hideaway. You quickly shove items into these spaces and shut the door behind you before they spill out.

6. You accrue late fees on bills because you don't reconcile your financial statements.

7. Spaces in your home can't be utilized for their intended purpose.

8. Areas of your home can't be cleaned properly because they're cluttered.

9.  Disorganization is causing conflicts in your relationships with friends and family, or causing you to decline invitations because you feel tied to your home.
10. You find yourself running out of space, even though your amount of storage space hasn't been reduced by a major event like welcoming a new baby or moving into a smaller home.

## How do I know if I would be classified as a compulsive hoarder?

Compulsive hoarding is more than simply being disorganized. Most of us associate hoarding with stories we've heard about people whose homes have only narrow pathways through stacks of junk, or about people who have fifty cats. But compulsive hoarding is a medical condition in which someone is incapable of parting with items, including true junk. Here are the top four behaviors of compulsive hoarders.

1.  The person holds on to items, planning to use them later. However, he or she never uses them. These are items that most people would not consider to be useful or valuable and have no trouble parting with, such as:

    • Junk mail
    • Outdated catalogs or newspapers
    • Items purchased for others as gifts but never given away
    • Clothing that doesn't fit
    • Out-of-control collections, like knickknacks, that overtake a space
    • Broken things, including cars in the driveway
    • Free items just because they are free

2. The home or parts of the home are too cluttered to use for their intended purpose.

   - Dining room tables that can't be used for dining
   - Kitchen countertops that can't be used for cooking
   - Couches that can't be used for sitting
   - Beds that can't be used for sleeping
   - Garages that can't be used for parking cars
   - Showers that can't be used for showering
   - Car seats that can't be used for passengers
   - Floors that can't be walked on
   - Exits that are blocked

3. Utilities, like lights, are disconnected simply because the person misplaced and did not pay the bills. The person's credit scores are adversely affected by late payments. Bank accounts are overdrawn because the person is unable to reconcile and record deposits and withdrawals.

4. The person suffers from a considerable amount of distress or isolation due to the clutter. For example, the person can't invite friends or family to the home because he or she is so embarrassed by the clutter. For the same reason, repairs can't be made because the person won't let repair or maintenance professionals into the home. Shades are kept drawn so that nobody can see the clutter inside. Family members argue about the clutter. The person also might suffer from depression or anxiety because of the clutter.

If you exhibit signs of hoarding and want help, seek treatment from a therapist who specializes in obsessive-compulsive disorder and hoarding issues.

## Can clutter be a safety concern?

Yes, absolutely, and not in just the obvious ways. We tend to think of piles of clutter on a staircase as being a hazard. While that is true, in more extreme clutter cases people have a hard time walking normally through a room without the risk of tripping or bumping into things. The safety of children is another concern, as piles of items or overloaded furniture might topple on them. In some cases young children are confined to a very small play area or to a playpen because being on the floor is a danger. Cluttered homes can be at risk for fire or insect/vermin infestation, and health problems can arise when areas of the home can't be cleaned properly. A cluttered car can lead to an accident if the driver is distracted by items falling off the seat or dashboard, or if an object rolls on the floor and wedges itself by the gas and brake pedals.

## Is it true that having perfectionist tendencies can actually lead to disorganization?

I know it sounds counterintuitive, but it is true. Perfectionists tend to have an all-or-nothing attitude. Perfectionists are unable to do a less-than-perfect job and their goals are often unrealistic and unattainable. So, often they opt to do nothing at all. For example, to tackle a disorganized linen closet, a perfectionist won't simply refold a few towels to make some space. Instead, he or she might plan to get the perfect shelf divider, buy new shelf paper, and research whether folding or rolling towels is best. As a result, the project becomes overwhelming, the linen closet gets messier, and the perfectionist feels defeated. The solution for the perfectionist is to lower the bar and plan to do a portion of the job now and the rest later. Most likely, later will never come, but that's just fine. Since perfectionists do such a great job, the first round is bound to be enough.

## Free items or sale items aren't really clutter, are they?

They can be. Any item you have but do not use translates to clutter. When things are on sale our instinct is to buy a lot—logically, it sounds like a good way to save. But that is rarely the case. When you buy more items than you need, can use, or have room to store, you haven't saved. Think about a skirt you might have purchased from the clearance rack. It was originally part of a set but the top is missing, and that's why it was such a steal. If you can't locate a top that matches the skirt, you won't be able to wear it, which means you wasted your money.

Free things really do have a cost. Sure, a few free promotional mugs and key chains picked up along the way may not seem that bad, but since you didn't make an effort to buy them, you probably did not need them. Chances are you won't use them that often, or at all, but you still have to store them and spend time cleaning around them. Plus, they take up valuable space where something you do use and love could go.

## Did I inherit my disorganization?

I'm often asked if there is a disorganization (or organization) gene. While I'm not a geneticist, I do know that all people are born with gifts and talents. Some are talented singers, others are gifted painters, and, yes, some have a more developed skill for putting things in their place. These are the people who are often called natural born organizers. Fortunately, even if you were not blessed with an aptitude for organization, you can cultivate it just like any other talent. And just like any other talent, the more you practice, the better you get. If you did not happen to grow up in a home where organizational skills were reinforced, it's not too late. Instead of blaming your situation on the lack of a role model, you can spend your energy on learning and practicing organizational skills. Though you may never be the world's best organizer, you can be happy with how you maintain your surroundings.

## I used to be super-organized; now I can't even find my keys. What happened?

Something changed, causing you to change from organized to not so organized. You usually can find the reason for your change outside of the clutter. For example, grief over the loss of a loved one might make it impossible for you to go through the person's belongings or part with his or her stuff. Medical conditions like depression or attention deficit disorder (ADD) can also cause a change in organizational ability. Other medical situations, like surgery or injuries from a car accident, can leave you less mobile and physically incapable of staying organized. Other situations that can bring about a setback in organizational abilities are caring for an elderly parent or ill spouse, moving to a new home, changing jobs, introducing a new child into your home, and disasters like a fire or a flood. The good news is that many of these situations are temporary. Though you'll most likely never go back to your old organizational habits, you can develop new ways of organizing that work for your current lifestyle.

## What's the best test for assessing how organized I am?

While there is no specific test to gauge your level of organization (or lack thereof) one way to check your skills is to ask, "Can I find what I need when I need it?" Ask yourself this question throughout the day. The faster you can find an item, the more organized the space is. Think about something like your keys. Are they always in the same place so you can find them easily? Or do you have to search for them because you never put them in the same spot? Which of these items could you find in less than two minutes?

- Passport
- Sunglasses
- Band-Aids
- Pen with ink in it
- Last year's tax return
- Grocery shopping list
- Library book that is due

The more you can locate, the more organized you are.

## When will I finally be organized?

The reality is that there will always be more to organize; you will never "finally" be organized. You will always need to organize new stuff and maintain the organization of old stuff. As you are sorting today's mail, tomorrow's mail is already on its way. If you keep thinking that complete organization will happen someday, you're setting yourself up for disappointment. Instead, be realistic and create simple systems that will help you to stay organized today and in the future.

## What are the root causes of disorganization?

Here are seven basic causes of disorganization:

1.  A lack of good habits. There are no elementary school classes on clutter control. If no one teaches you how to do something, how can you be expected to learn?
2.  A lack of respect for belongings. Usually, this stems from a childhood where your personal possessions were treated as easily replaceable, or other people picked up after you.
3.  A need for more time. This is a legitimate concern that sometimes is used as an excuse.

4. Rebelling. At some point we all want to place our hands on our hips and yell, "You can't make me if I don't want to!"

5. Perfectionism. There's nothing wrong with wanting to do a great job. The challenge comes when the fantasy of a project done perfectly causes a paralyzing fear that results in inaction.

6. Procrastination. Putting off small tasks like sorting the mail or putting the dirty dishes in the dishwasher always leads to a bigger and more overwhelming mess later on.

7. A setback or major life change. This might explain why someone who once was very organized suddenly battles clutter and disorganization.

## Can clutter affect my well-being?

Yes, without a doubt. Here are the areas where clutter can be a factor in your health and well-being:

### Family and relationships

Clutter in the house can cause irritability, resentment, and stress among family members. These feelings can lead to temper tantrums, outbursts, and overall disharmony—especially if one is frustrated by other people's clutter. If you can't organize your home, you may believe you aren't a good person or aren't a good example for your kids. Excessive clutter can cause depression, acting out, and bad behavior in children due to their inability to focus.

Searching for your keys or an item of clothing can make you chronically late for events or appointments, which in turn can affect your social life. Clutter also keeps you from getting close to people, because you don't want people to visit your home.

## Mental health

Excessive clutter often causes feelings of shame, guilt, anger, and embarrassment. Clutter drains your energy. Think of how you feel when you see a stack of old magazines to sort or a pile of mending you've been putting off. When items go unused, unloved, and uncared for, their stagnant energy may affect your energy. A lack of organizational skills may make you feel inadequate, but many people struggle with clutter.

The stress caused by clutter can be daunting. Every time you can't find something, you argue with a loved one, or you can't relax because you're worrying about how to clear the clutter, your stress level increases.

## Illness

When cluttered areas of the home can't be properly cleaned, dust, mold, and mildew can build up and cause or exacerbate health problems for those who live there. Sinus problems and allergies are linked to an accumulation of allergens and dust in uncleaned rooms. Stress caused by clutter can lower your immunity, so you may have frequent, persistent colds or other infections. Clutter can also make it more difficult to eat healthy, resulting in headaches, fatigue, or weight gain.

## Time

Having too much stuff eats up your time. Everything you own requires some amount of care and organization, which takes time. Trying to take care of a large amount of stuff often leads to procrastination and tardiness, which in turn wastes your and other people's time.

## Your future

Holding on to clutter often grounds you in the past, at the cost of your present life and your future. Clutter distracts you from thinking about your goals, completing projects, and having hobbies. Things from your past remind you of what you used to like to do, leaving little or no time for the things you use and love today.

### Hygiene

When the home is really messy, it can be difficult to locate clean clothing or find the time to do the wash. Some people even store items in the shower, making it difficult, if not impossible, to take a shower. Extreme disorganization can make it a challenge to locate everyday items like deodorant or toothpaste, or to gauge when more needs to be purchased.

## Can clutter affect my body weight?

Yes. If you find it difficult to lose weight, clutter might be a contributing factor. You might lack time to work out or get to the gym because your home is disorganized. If you use your home exercise equipment as an expensive clothes hanger, or if clutter prevents you from getting to the equipment, you might be unable to exercise. Dealing with clutter day after day can drain your energy, making you less active. It can also stunt your ability to create healthy meals. You might not have enough room to prepare food in the kitchen, you might not have the time to organize before you can cook, the pantry might not be stocked, or you might not remember to defrost foods ahead of time. Without a healthy meal plan, it becomes easier to pick up fast food, which is not as healthy as something you'd have prepared at home. Finally, if you feel guilty or depressed about the clutter, you may opt for unhealthy snacks for comfort.

## I feel isolated and lonely; could that be due to the clutter?

Yes, one of the side effects of disorganization is an inability to socialize. You tend to not invite people to your home or don't allow them to drop by without calling first. As a result, you strain valuable connections with friends and family. When you stop socializing, you might get a little less meticulous about your appearance. You might not care about what you choose to wear or how you style your hair. That can make you ashamed about your appearance, causing further isolation. If you feel isolated or lonely, start reconnecting with people by asking a friend or family member to join you in an outing this week.

## Can my attitude affect my ability to organize?

Yes, attitude has a lot to do with organization. If you think you can, then you can—and if you think you can't, you're absolutely right. Your attitude is everything, so try to keep it as positive as possible. If you think your family won't help you organize, then chances are they won't. Or you'll be so focused on noticing whenever they don't help that you'll never realize when they do pitch in. Maintaining a positive attitude is not always easy, especially when you're faced with a mountain of laundry or a garage full of junk. But the job will be ten times harder if you focus on the negative. Finding something enjoyable—or at least bearable—about the task of organizing can make all the difference in the world.

## I simply lack the energy to get started. How can I get motivated?

Getting started is often the most difficult part. The trick is to take the smallest possible step forward. Choose a tiny task—something that seems too small to be a real task, like locating just one item to donate to a local charity. Once you accomplish that one task, the next step reveals itself and you're on a roll. Seeing progress will energize you and give you the momentum you need to continue.

# Why am I so organized at work but not at home?

There are a few reasons for this. The good news is that no matter what the reason, you can make your house run as efficiently as your office. Here are some reasons why your office may be tidier than your home:

- Your coworkers and superiors can see your mess at work, and your reputation is at stake.
- You might have more to lose if you are disorganized at work. You might lose a raise due to a poor rating on your annual performance review, lose a bonus or promotion, or lose your status on a big project. Your job may be on the line if you can't work productively and meet time lines.
- You might be able to delegate organizing to other people at work.
- At the office there might be systems in place that you have to follow.
- You might have more energy to stay organized in the daytime; when you get home in the evening you're simply burnt out.
- Most likely you are not emotionally attached to the stuff you have at work. I bet you're not all that sentimental about the latest spreadsheet you created.
- At the office you might be held accountable for keeping things neat and filed so coworkers can locate them. At home nobody needs you to put stuff back, or else.
- You might receive acknowledgment for a job well done at the office; this usually is not the case at home.
- You might be less comfortable with the people at work, so you give more thought to making a good impression. At home your comfort level allows your messy side to show.

## I seem to sabotage myself when trying to get organized. Why?

You might find clutter to be a useful distraction. The most common reasons for keeping clutter are:

- It can be uncomfortable to have free time or free space. When your life is organized you might start to think about things in a new and deeper way. You'll have the time, energy, and space to get to know yourself better and to forge deeper relationships with those around you. If that feels uncomfortable, then maybe worrying about clutter is your way of not going to that place.
- It might be comforting to look around and see all your possessions, all the things you worked hard to obtain. The items actually can become a part of your identity. After all, who are you without all that stuff?
- As much as you believe you want people to visit your home, your actions speak louder if you keep your house so messy that you cannot entertain. Although you may have an abundance of entertaining ware, you'll never have a chance to use it unless you get organized enough to have company. Since it may have been some time since you last had guests over, it can also feel uncomfortable to have people in your home. You might have problems socializing or be ashamed of the state of your home.
- If you share the cluttered space with someone you resent, you might be keeping things messy to vent your anger at him or her, especially if that person likes things more organized.

## Could the fact that I'm easily distracted be caused by clutter?

Yes, clutter can distract even the most focused people, myself included. If you're trying to remember all you have to do and you see projects everywhere that need your attention, it's no wonder that you veer off track. You might find yourself working on something and then a thought pops into your head, making you switch tasks. When you're distracted you're not focusing on the task at hand, so you work more slowly. You might not pay enough attention to remember the details. For example, if while organizing your home office, you start thinking about the newsletter you need to type for your club, you might misfile papers, forget where you placed things, and even accidentally shred important documents. It would be better to stop organizing the office for a moment to jot down newsletter ideas, and then get back to organizing instead of trying to divide your brainpower.

## My home is so cluttered that I don't like being there. What can I do?

Let me assure you that this situation is common and fixable. Avoiding your home can become an escape from the suffocating feeling of a cluttered home. The catch is that if you are away from home, you might go shopping and buy more things, which only exacerbates the problem. Making a new purchase may give you a sense of excitement, but that feeling is short-lived. When you return home with your purchase, reality hits. The best compromise in this situation is to first organize one area of your home. Then, if you simply must, reward yourself with a trip to a store to buy one special piece for the newly organized space. Chances are you'll find yourself buying less because you value the freedom that comes with empty space. The best advice is to start with a small organizational task. For example, organize the kitchen counter and then buy a decorative oil and spice jar to display. Or reorganize your closet by donating unused clothes to charity. Then treat yourself to a new outfit.

## Is it possible to save money by getting organized?

Not only is it possible—it's practically unavoidable. Disorganization is expensive in many ways. Here are the top twenty:

1. Fees: Late fees for bills paid past the deadline, or overdraft fees in your checking account
2. Rush charges: Having to overnight a mortgage payment or holiday gifts to out-of-state family because you waited too long
3. Wasted memberships or subscriptions: Delivered newspapers you do not have time to read or a yoga class membership you rarely use
4. Overpaying: Buying a gift and then paying to have it wrapped at the store, when you could just wrap it yourself with the wrapping paper you have at home
5. Financial penalties: Missing a deadline for paying back an IRA loan or failing to pay taxes on time
6. Lost raises: Being overlooked for a promotion because you were so disorganized you missed a deadline or forgot to call a potential client
7. A lowered credit score: Paying bills late, or applying for too many credit cards because you can't keep track of how many you have
8. Partial reimbursements: Returning an item without a receipt and getting only a partial credit, missing the deadline to return an item for a full refund, or simply not returning the item at all
9. Lost money: A birthday check that you never cashed, a misplaced paycheck that you never deposited, a gift card that you never redeemed, or store credits that you never used
10. Expired coupons: Coupons that you clipped but never redeemed
11. Moving: Moving into a larger home because you outgrew your old space

12. Double buying: For example, buying another black T-shirt because you forgot you already own one
13. Rebuying: Purchasing another Halloween costume for your child because you can't find the one you already own
14. Overbuying: Purchasing a case of canned soup but not consuming it all by the expiration date
15. Storage: Spending money on offsite storage or in-home storage, which can cost thirty dollars per square foot
16. Children: Having to hire a tutor for your child because he or she can't study or complete homework due to disorganization
17. Stress: Being stressed by disorganization, leading to headaches or other physical ailments requiring medication or other treatment
18. Medical bills: Tripping over clutter and getting injured, suffering from allergies or asthma because you can't properly clean your home
19. Therapy: Paying for marriage counseling because you and your spouse disagree about how a home is maintained, or paying for a divorce if the issues can't be resolved
20. Lost time: Time is priceless, so this is the most expensive of all

## Is disorganization simply a bad habit?

It's true that good habits like putting things back where they belong when you're finished using them wards off disorganization. At the same time, poor habits like placing items on horizontal surfaces instead of their proper place contribute tremendously to being disorganized. But disorganization is not solely a product of bad habits; you can have great habits and still have clutter. Organization systems that work for you in conjunction with good habits are the keys to success.

## Are horizontal surfaces a bad idea?

Yes. Horizontal surfaces act as magnets for all sorts of stuff. Think of any flat surface in your home or office—it's bound to be a resting place for dropped items. Horizontal surfaces usually are wasted space. For example, the top of a three-shelf bookcase is about waist-high, creating a prime horizontal space for clutter. A vertical piece of furniture like a floor-to-ceiling bookcase not only eliminates the tempting drop zone but also doubles the amount of storage space.

## Can furniture choices affect my level of organization?

Furniture choices have a lot to do with organization or lack thereof. Furniture can be easy to use (or not), and it can offer proper storage (or not). If you like a piece of furniture and it's easy to use, you'll use it. If you don't like it, you probably won't use it. Freshly laundered clothes will find it hard to find their way from the laundry basket to a dresser whose drawers are hard to open. A closet with ample storage space like shelving and bars for hanging, on the other hand, will make storing and retrieving clothes a snap. Multifunctional furniture is also important, especially in a small space. A typical living room end table can be swapped with a small chest of drawers. The drawers offer storage space for remote controls, magazines, and more, while those items would have collected on the top of an end table, causing clutter.

## How long will it take me to get organized?

That depends on two things: the amount and type of items you have to organize, plus how ready and focused you are to get the job done. Someone who is really motivated, can work without getting distracted, and has just a few piles of stuff to organize will probably be done in an hour or two. But someone who has a four-drawer file cabinet full of papers to organize, and who stops to read every clipped article or to reminisce over photographs before deciding what to keep, will take much longer. Remember that getting the space organized is not the end of the story—staying organized is an ongoing process that is never complete. Every day you have more items like mail, email, and new purchases to sort and store. If you never make time to discard items, they will quickly overrun your home or office. The good news is that once you have a home for everything, putting items away is no more than a ten-minute job every day, even less if you always put things back when you're done with them.

## Is a home truly a reflection of the person who lives there?

Absolutely. The items in a home reflect the past and present interests of the people who live there, plus their dreams and plans for the future. A home can provide clues to its residents' health and state of happiness. Take a moment to look around your home. What books are on the bookshelves? Those books usually reflect the interests of someone in the home. Are there mostly cookbooks or gardening books or maybe books on how to clear clutter? If most are cookbooks, that's a dead giveaway that someone who lives there loves to cook. The pantry and refrigerator also can reveal a lot about the inhabitants. If there are take-out containers in the refrigerator, that likely means someone doesn't have time to cook. A closet full of high-end suits can indicate that a person has a job outside the home.

## How can I ensure success or at least better my odds of getting organized?

To ensure a higher success rate, set small, achievable goals for yourself. When we have unrealistic expectations, we set ourselves up to fail. Avoid taking on too much, like saying yes to every volunteer opportunity, planning to organize a whole room in one hour, and expecting to get a three-page to-do list done by the end of the day. There are only twenty-four hours in the day, and you are only one person. Plan manageable goals for the day. I suggest five tasks above and beyond your regular routine. Those five could be something like calling to make an appointment for your dog at the veterinarian, going to the post office, wrapping gifts for an upcoming party, spending twenty minutes organizing the linen closet, and returning a phone call to your doctor's office. These are tasks you can actually accomplish. If you have spare time when you're done, you can start on tomorrow's list or take a break. Either way, you'll feel great!

## Is there any way to avoid feeling defeated at the end of the day?

Instead of recounting all that did not go well and everything you did not accomplish that day, simply give yourself a pat on the back for getting through the day and consider the things that did go well. We get more of what we focus on, so if you dwell on how busy you are and how much more there is to do, then that will become true. However, if you are grateful to have been blessed with another day and you feel good about having read another page in this book, remembering to pick the kids up from school on time, and sorting the mail, then you'll feel happy and successful. Sure, there's more to do, but that's a good thing—it means you are alive and doing things. Quite frankly, the alternative is not all that appealing.

## How can I stop losing things the minute I put them down?

Chances are you're always putting things down in a different spot that may be covered in clutter. If you place a pen by a pile of magazines and newspapers, it most likely will disappear under the pile. If you've placed your glasses down ten times today—each time in a different location—it's no wonder you can't find them again or even remember where you put them. Having a designated spot for important everyday items can be a huge time and frustration saver. This might mean having a spot in each room for items like reading glasses and pens, so you have a designated spot for them as you wander from room to room. You might try a single decorative basket in the living room, bedroom, and kitchen. The basket is used only for reading glasses, notepaper, and pens. Get in the habit of placing them in the basket, and you'll always find them there.

## Will increasing my memory help me get organized?

Not exactly. We can only remember so many things. There is probably nothing wrong with your memory other than it has reached its capacity. Trying to remember too many things at once (e.g., what to buy at the grocery store, who to call, when to pay your bills, what to cook for dinner every night this week, your doctor appointment, and the deadline for the volunteer project) is extremely difficult. Some things are bound to slip through the cracks. So instead of trying to remember more, remember less. Find a portable-size spiral-bound notebook, and use it as the one place you make notes to yourself. Give the notebook a home so you are confident you won't misplace it. Fill the notebook with notes, lists, and reminders. Anything that is date-related should be written on your calendar, and you should check your calendar every evening as you prepare for the next day. By writing down what's important rather than trying to remember it, you'll eliminate a lot of mental clutter and free up your brainpower for other things.

## Why do I have conversations or internal debates with myself?

Do your conversations go something like this? You go shopping and your purchase comes in a big bag with a rope handle. You think to yourself: "I should keep this bag. It's a nice bag with a sturdy handle, and I can use it to carry something one day. It's nicer than the bag I get at that other store. Maybe I should keep this one and toss the other one, or maybe just keep both, because I might need them both. I could use the not-so-nice one to send stuff home with someone else, and keep this one for myself. I think I'll put them both in my special bag collection. Where did I put that bag collection? Last I saw it, it was in the front hall closet, but then I moved it when company was coming. This bag is big; maybe I can put the whole collection in this bag. Yep, I'm going to keep it." Please know this type of inner conversation is not uncommon, and there is nothing wrong with you. The best way to avoid these odd and time-consuming debates with yourself is to set "par level." You can read more about par levels on page 60.

## Why does clutter make me feel so guilty?

Staring at piles of unaccomplished tasks is not a great feeling. It can trigger many emotions, including guilt. You might wonder, "How did I let it get this bad?" "Why can't I keep everything neat and clean?" "Am I passing down these habits to my children?" "There must be something wrong with me." Other negative thoughts and feelings may surface, too. I can assure you that you are not alone, and that by simply taking a small action you can shift those feelings from negative to positive.

## Does clutter affect my mood?

Without a doubt, clutter has a lot to do with your mood. Think about a day when you woke up and breezed out the door on time because your outfit was ready, your bag was packed, and your car keys were on the hook by the door, ready to go. Most likely, you arrived at work happy and calm. Now think about a day when you woke up, had to find and iron an outfit to wear, realized you were out of milk for your cereal, struggled to find your car keys, and ended up being late to work. You were not as happy that day. When you're more organized, you tend to feel energetic, positive, happy, successful, satisfied, social, harmonious, clearheaded, and creative. When you're less organized you tend to feel rushed, stressed, unhappy, frustrated, overwhelmed, dissatisfied, antisocial, tired, and argumentative.

## Why do I feel like I need permission to let go of things?

Sometimes we simply get stuck. We may be unsure of the right decision and don't want to make a mistake we'll regret later. For example, if you refinance a mortgage, you might wonder whether you need to save all of the paperwork. We want someone else to tell us it is okay to let something go. Perhaps you have something others would keep, such as your child's first tooth. You might be ready to part with it but wonder if that makes you a bad mom. If you're debating about getting rid of something, I give you permission to let it go. Free yourself from the burden and allow that newly found space to attract something new to your life.

## I always second-guess myself and talk myself into keeping things. What can I do?

The "what if I need this?" question seems to stem from a fear of the unknown. You're not sure what the future holds, so to be prepared you'll keep everything. The trouble with that is you probably won't remember everything you keep, won't have room to store it, or won't be able to find it should the need arise. To determine if you truly need something, start by asking yourself a few basic questions:

- Do I have something else that does the same job?
- Can I get this again if I need it?
- Am I really going to make the time to use this in the next six months?
- Will this be out of date by the time I get to it?
- Is there someone else who could use this now?
- Does it work, do I have all the pieces, and do I know how to use it?
- If I only had one hour to pack and move as many of my belongings as I could, would I pack it?
- What's the worst thing that could happen if I let this go?

It usually is easier to let something go if you know it is going to someone who can benefit from it right now. Remember that when you hold on to things just because they might be useful in the future, you lose out on living in the present. You're so busy collecting items and storing them for possible future use, you waste time, energy, and money. What's more, the space for your passions is taken up by boxes of stuff that might (or might not) become a future need.

## Chapter 2 — GETTING STARTED

- What's a quick and easy way of organizing?
- If I plan to get back to something later, do I still need to put it away when I'm done with it?
- What's the best way to successfully complete a long-term organizing project?
- What's the best way to make a habit out of organizing?
- I have a very hard time parting with things. What can I do to overcome my separation anxiety?
- Is there such a thing as being too sentimental? I can't seem to bear to part with mementos and special objects.
- Some areas of my home always attract clutter. What should I do?
- My stuff is spread out all over my house. Should I bring the items together to organize, or organize as I go along?
- What can I do to motivate others and myself to get organized?
- Is January the best time to make a resolution to get organized?
- What if I'm waiting for a special occasion to use the "good" stuff I've stored?
- How can I get to all the fix-it projects I keep putting off?
- Can I organize the wrong way?
- Why is it the minute I let something go, I find a use for it?
- What if I'm afraid that the end result of my organizing will not match my expectations?
- Do disorganized people have different traits and issues?
- Is it true I should just decide to decide?
- I'm waiting to "get to it later," but later never comes. What am I doing wrong?
- How do I know if I'm ready to hire a professional organizer?
- How do I find professional organizers in my area?
- What services does a professional organizer offer?
- How much does a professional organizer cost?
- What questions should I ask when interviewing an organizer?
- I'd like to hire a professional organizer, but what if I'm too embarrassed to let someone see my mess?
- Should I hire a professional organizer to help someone else who is disorganized?
- Why hire a professional organizer?

## What's a quick and easy way of organizing?

"Brownie organizing" is a quick and easy method I developed based on the directions on a box of brownie mix—three simple steps, with a suggested bake time of just fifteen to twenty-five minutes. When baking, you need to set a timer to cook the brownies just right. After you eat them you'll probably want to make more at some point. This is my way of organizing: I have just three simple steps, I work in short lengths of time, and I set a timer to stay focused and on track. And when I'm finished, I want to do more organizing.

The three steps to organize any space are:

1. Work in small blocks of time, sorting out one area and grouping similar items.
2. Put away only the items you use and love, or what the IRS says you must keep. Find really good homes for all the other stuff.
3. Keep the newly organized space, well, organized.

I don't recommend waiting for an entire free day to get organized because it never happens. You'll never find that kind of time. If you have a busy schedule, you usually can carve out only a short block of time—like fifteen to twenty-five minutes. Set a timer to help stay on track, and you'll use that time wisely. In most cases the project will not be complete by the time the time is up, but you'll have made noticeable progress. The goal is to work for the block of time, not to finish. Once you complete this block of time, make another block of time to make even more progress.

## If I plan to get back to something later, do I still need to put it away when I'm done with it?

Yes, put it away anyway. When I say to put it away when you are done, I don't mean when you're done using it forever; I mean when you're done using it for the moment. Even if you plan to come back to the item later, your plans may get sidetracked and the item will get mixed up with other stuff. If you're reading the newspaper at the kitchen table, for example, and then decide to cook breakfast, you first should put the paper away. Even though you plan to get back to reading it later, in the meantime it will consume your kitchen table. Unfinished projects quickly make a mess of your space. Clean up as you go—you can always retrieve the item later. When you do, you'll know right where to find that item and have a clean space in which to enjoy it.

## What's the best way to successfully complete a long-term organizing project?

Plan for multiple organizing sessions, and then stop each session before finishing what you're working on, leaving the rest for next time. This might sound backward, but it actually works. When you leave a project knowing the next step you need to take when you resume, you'll be more anxious to get back to work and know right where to start. For example, a long-term project like organizing a wardrobe closet will require at least a few sessions. If you work until you are burned out and then just walk away, when you come back you'll have to remember where you left off. On the other hand, if you stop before doing that "one last thing," chances are you'll be anxious to get back to it. Leave yourself a note to remind you where you stopped, in case it may be some time before you return to the project.

## What's the best way to make a habit out of organizing?

Consider your new organizing systems to be new house rules. Post them if you like, and get all family members to agree to them. Once everyone is on board, the new systems will become a way of life. Make sure that someone supports you and keeps you accountable, too. By connecting with others who are also trying to stay organized you can share success stories, vent, and exchange helpful tips.

Also set aside time during your week for maintenance. Just as you make time for errands, shopping, cooking, and cleaning, you also need time for keeping things organized. You might spend fifteen minutes one week touching up the linen closet or twenty minutes one weekend filing new paperwork. Blocking off time on your calendar for maintaining organization reduces your chances of falling behind.

## I have a very hard time parting with things. What can I do to overcome my separation anxiety?

Here are the top reasons we become too attached to our stuff, and what we can do about it.

### What if I want it later?

Have you heard the old standby, "If you haven't used it in a season, just let it go?" If you're fearful of parting with something even though you haven't used it, then try thinking about it this way: Items you are not using are taking up space and preventing you from using the items you do love. When you let go of what is less important, you're able to enjoy things that have been waiting for you.

An effective way to overcome fear is to challenge it. Think about how you'll feel when you challenge yourself to part with something. It will feel less overwhelming if you let go little by little. Practice parting with one thing at a time. Each time you let go of something will be a little easier than the time before, and soon you'll be less fearful. Be aware that often it isn't the clutter that controls us, but our doubts and fears. By parting with items gradually, you'll start to trust yourself more and feel more confident about your decisions. Trust that if you make a "wrong" decision by tossing something out, you'll still live. You can find a substitute, buy another one, etc. Parting with clutter is not a life-or-death situation. So go ahead, toss something out. See how you feel. Chances are you'll feel empowered rather than weakened.

### But it's a memory

When trying to part with things, be selectively sentimental. If you keep everything, your precious memories will be lost among the clutter. Choose a treasure box and keep a few items. If an item is too large to fit in the box, take a photo of it and keep only the photo. Give the rest of the items to someone who will use them. Another thought is to use the items in an unusual way. For example, have a seamstress make a blanket from squares of baby clothes, or a tooth fairy pillow from a christening gown. Remember that many treasured items are ruined in storage anyway. They yellow, become brittle, or are damaged by humidity or moisture. So use them—don't lose them.

### I'm going to fix it one day

You might have a dream of fixing broken items someday. Many times it costs more to fix something than replace it. Plus, it takes a lot of time to fix things. A good way to deal with this situation is to give yourself a deadline for broken items to be fixed. If the deadline isn't met, discard them.

### It was a gift

Someone has probably given you an unwanted gift. There is no polite way to refuse, so you likely accepted it even though you didn't want it. But remember that if you don't like something, it will drag down your spirits every time you look at it. So dump the guilt and give the gift to someone who will use it and love it, by donating it to a charity, for example. If the gift giver ever asks you where the item is, you can say you enjoyed it, then passed it on so someone else could enjoy it.

### Information overload

Be ruthless with paper. Paper is like peaches—you don't want to keep either around too long. No one has time to read everything, and most information is available in another form, like online. Put junk mail straight into the recycling bin. When a new magazine or catalog arrives, recycle the old one, read or unread.

The best way to overcome separation anxiety with clutter is to give it a deadline.

You now have specific solutions for letting items go. However, clutter usually will stay put until one of two things occurs: You're finally ready to deal with the clutter because you just can't stand it anymore, or you have a real deadline—houseguests, a party, moving, remodeling, etc. A deadline is more likely to generate action than anything else.

## Is there such a thing as being too sentimental? I can't seem to bear to part with mementos and special objects.

Yes, it is possible to be too attached to special objects. Keeping these objects can make you feel stressed if they're too difficult to store or you're running out of space.

Remember that if you keep too many mementos, they will be lost among the mess. Treat your special items with the respect they deserve. Try to overcome your separation anxiety by taking a photo of the item and then donating the item to a charity, where it can continue to have a life. That will make you feel better than keeping the special item in the back of a closet or a musty basement.

## Some areas of my home always attract clutter. What should I do?

Create storage places in those areas. Items typically are dropped because they either don't have a home or their home isn't convenient. If a person walks into your home and drapes his or her jacket across the back of a nearby chair, decide where you'd prefer that jacket to go. If most visitors enter through your house's side door, that means the front hall closet is out of the way. A fix might be to hang a few pegs near the side door and implement a new routine of hanging jackets there. By creating a storage option right where it is needed, the person can't help but put his or her things away.

Another way to solve this problem is to eliminate as many horizontal surfaces as possible. Horizontal surfaces are just an invitation to set things down. If you can't eliminate the surface, at least fill it temporarily with decorative or breakable items to remind people to place their items elsewhere. Next, add storage space. In the living room, ottomans with lift-off lids serve as storage spots as well as extra seating. A floor-to-ceiling bookshelf, baskets, or hooks on the walls are other ideas.

## My stuff is spread out all over my house. Should I bring the items together to organize, or organize as I go along?

This is a classic question. Without a doubt, it is best to organize as you go. The time it would take to gather all the items is better spent actually organizing. The trick here is to create temporary solutions as you organize. Don't invest in storage options since you're not sure how much you'll find or need to store. For example, if you have photos stashed in boxes and drawers all over your home, start small. Find a single box to store a handful of photos. Sort the photos by category chronologically, then add more as you find them.

Eventually you'll have a good amount of photos in the box. Then it's time to move them into a photo-safe box or into albums if that is your plan. If you had waited to start organizing photos until you located all the photos in your home, you probably would never get started. Or if you did locate all the photos first, the mountain of photos would be so overwhelming you'd likely give up. Sorting as you go is sure to lead to success.

## What can I do to motivate others and myself to get organized?

We all need a little push sometimes. Here are some things you can do to inspire everyone to get organized:

- Make it a family affair: Everyone pitches in for a specific amount of time. After that, the family does something fun together.
- Money motivates: Make a "for sale" pile. After you sell those items, distribute the proceeds to individuals or use the money for an outing.
- Game time: Turn the cleanup into a game. Set a timer and see who can clean up the most before the bell rings.
- Make it fun: Play music while cleaning or make a special cleanup trail mix to munch on.
- Social organizing: Invite a trusted friend over to offer support or actually roll up her sleeves and help out.
- Make a date: You'll be motivated to organize your home if you've sent out party invitations to host a party.
- Make a compromise: When you're done organizing, you get to repaint the room or buy that new slipcover you've been eyeing.
- Tell someone: Sometimes all it takes is going public. We all tend to be more willing to do things for other people before we'd do it for ourselves. So once you tell someone you're going to do

something, you will—especially if you trust the person to help hold you accountable.

- Spa day: Most of us would be more than willing to clean out the garage if we knew a spa day was booked for the following day. Not a fan of going to the spa? Just plan something you love to do.
- Find support: Connect with others who have the same mission and can hold you accountable while offering tips and motivation. Something like a Clutter Club, clubs like these meet in person or over the phone and can be just the motivation you need.

## Is January the best time to make a resolution to get organized?

No, I'm not a big fan of New Year's resolutions made on January 1. Expecting to change routines overnight, right after a stressful time of year and without a clear plan is a recipe for disaster. How many times have we made a list of resolutions only to disappoint ourselves by mid-January? Along with the disappointment usually comes guilt. It's much more effective to make smaller changes over a period of time with support and a clear plan in place. Learning a single new routine can take close to a month. So choose one new goal and go for it. When you succeed, you'll repeat the process and be successful year-round.

## What if I'm waiting for a special occasion to use the "good" stuff I've stored?

Life is short, so I suggest using the "good" stuff today. In many cases, the good stuff is packed up and ruined in storage, we never think to bring it out and use it, or we never seem to have the right occasion to use it. Make today that special day to break out the good stuff and put it to use. You'll feel better having the items you love nearby, instead of hidden in a closet. Plus, you'll create new memories and pass down family history.

## How can I get to all the fix-it projects I keep putting off?

Try to fix an item right as soon as it breaks instead of leaving it for later. Often, it takes a lot less time to make repairs than you think. However, there will be times when fixing something immediately is impossible. When that's the case, collect what you need to make the repair. For a toy that needs batteries, locate the correct size, and if you need a mini screwdriver, grab that too. For broken glasses, find the itty-bitty screw and screwdriver. Keep all the parts together in a ziplock plastic bag. Then you'll have everything you need to complete the project the next time you sit down to watch television or while you are on the phone. Most of the time spent fixing something is really spent finding the parts you need to complete the project. If you make a fix-it caddy containing common items used for repairs, the next time you have a fix-it project you'll have a better chance of taking care of it on the spot.

## Can I organize the wrong way?

No, there is no right or wrong way to organize. You can decide to keep something and then change your mind and toss it. You can move items around. You can put items in storage into new containers. You can always change your mind. The only case where changing your mind isn't possible is when you opt to shred, toss, or donate items that can't be replaced. These days, however, many things are replaceable—just check online auction sites. You also can use the maybe box (see page 57) as a safety net.

## Why is it the minute I let something go, I find a use for it?

Everyone wants to know the answer to this one! The truth is that you only thought of another use because you just saw the item and it is fresh in your mind. If you hadn't just seen that item, you probably wouldn't have remembered that you had it. It's similar to when you're thinking of buying a particular model of car. All of a sudden, you notice that model everywhere around town. When something is fresh in your mind, you tend to think of it more.

## What if I'm afraid that the end result of my organizing will not match my expectations?

It can be intimidating to start organizing if you have unrealistic expectations. Try lowering your standards, at least temporarily. Get the basic organizing done first. Later, you can perfect it to match your higher standards. You might find that "finished" is better than "perfect," and you'll be thrilled with the results even though they may not be what you originally set out to accomplish. Remember almost everything can be changed, so if you're stuck on which shelving unit to buy or which shade of green paint to choose, just make a choice. You'll feel better once you do. You might just love what you chose and if not, you can change it later.

## Do disorganized people have different traits and issues?

Yes, there are seven basic types of organizing personalities. Use this list to identify your type, and then follow the specific solution given.

1.  Organizing product and tip junkie. You collect ideas and buy tools, but never actually do the work. Your solution: Stop buying and reading tips. Instead, set a timer for eighteen minutes and tackle a small project.

2. Last on the list. You organize everyone else in the house, but your stuff is a mess. Your solution: Realize that you are setting an example for everyone else, and that they need to become self-sufficient. Show them how to organize on their own and spend a little more time on your own stuff.

3. The keeper. You keep everything because it means something to you, you paid good money for it, it's still good, or you might use it one day. But keeping everything clutters up space, preventing you from using the stuff you love. Your solution: Work on items that have the least amount of meaning for you, and fill one bag with things you can give to a new home where they will be used and loved.

4. The last-minute emergency. The doorbell rings and you run around the house scooping up stuff and tossing it into baskets and bags. Then you stash the baskets or bags and greet your guests. Your solution: Plan ahead by breaking up a large clutter-clearing task into small jobs. Set a timer for eighteen minutes and go to work.

5. The procrastinator. You plan to spend some time de-cluttering but never seem to get around to it. Or you start by picking up an item but then put it down, unsure what to do with it. Your solution: Set a schedule by making clutter-clearing dates with yourself and writing them on the calendar. Work for a small block of time, and then give yourself a reward for a job well done. Your reward might be to watch a television show, have a special snack, have coffee with a friend, or relax and do nothing.

6. Driven to distraction. You set out to tackle an area and find something that belongs in another room. You bring it there, and while you're there get caught up doing something else,

leaving your original project undone. Your solution: Focus on the task at hand by making a pile of items to deliver somewhere else. Once the task is completed, distribute the items.

7. Perfection. You have a vision of what the space will look like, but there is no way you can live up to your high standard, so you do nothing. Your solution: Choose one small area and work on it. Resolve to make it good, and go back in your spare time to perfect it.

## Is it true I should just decide to decide?

I'm not sure; let me think about it (insert smile here.) Yes, in most cases *not* deciding is stressful, and almost all clutter comes from putting off making a decision. But if you simply make a decision, even if it's not the best decision, at least you've done *something*. Often not being able to make a choice is due to a lack of information that makes us fearful we'll make the wrong choice. So if you are not sure, just do something—make a choice you can change later or get more information, but take action. That's the most important part.

## I'm waiting to "get to it later," but later never comes. What am I doing wrong?

The only flaw with your plan is that you get busy and never get back to it. Maybe you put down the pile of mail to sort it later, you leave replying to emails until later, you stash a cardboard box in the garage to break it down for recycling later, and you are correct—later never comes. The key is to do it right then, otherwise it won't get done and it will be yet another to-do on your long list of to-dos. You don't need another task hanging over your head, so try wrapping it up in the moment.

## How do I know if I'm ready to hire a professional organizer?

It is becoming more commonplace to outsource your organizing to a professional. After all, you probably hire people to do other jobs you might not be skilled to do yourself, like cutting your hair or changing the oil in your car. Professional organizing is a job that has been on the rise since the mid-1980s. According to the National Association of Professional Organizers, there were just a handful of organizers in the country back then; today there are over 4,000 registered professional organizers. If you can answer yes to any of the following questions, then chances are you're ready to invest in a professional organizer.

1. Am I ready to team up with someone to make permanent changes in how I live?
2. Will I be able to put forth the effort and commitment this will take?
3. Do I have a budget set aside for this?
4. Can I be honest about what I use and don't use?
5. Am I willing to do the maintenance once I have a new system in place?
6. Am I tired of misplacing things and losing valuable time?
7. Am I ready to set a better example for those around me?

## How do I find professional organizers in my area?

There are a few different ways you can find local professional organizers. One is to do an online search. Type in the phrase "professional organizer + your town", and the search should result in a list of nearby organizers. You can also contact the National Association of Professional Organizers or, if you are in Canada, Professional Organizers in Canada, for a referral to an organizer in your area.

National Association of Professional Organizers
15000 Commerce Parkway, Suite C
Mount Laurel, NJ 08054
(856) 380-6828
http://www.napo.net

Professional Organizers in Canada
39 River Street
Toronto, Ontario M5A 3P1
http://www.organizersincanada.com

## What services does a professional organizer offer?

Professional organizers take a hands-on approach with their clients. That means hands-on, side-by-side sorting and de-cluttering of areas. Typically, the organizer tours the area and creates a plan, then the organizer and the client work in blocks of time to accomplish the goal. As an organizer sets up a new system for dealing with the client's belongings, he or she also helps the client determine what to keep, what to toss, and how to properly store items. In addition to organizing services for your home, some professional organizers also might organize your workplace. Other services might include:

- Accounting and bookkeeping
- Computer organizing and training
- Disaster preparedness
- Errands and personal shopping
- Event planning
- Filing
- Garage and estate sales
- Paying bills
- Photo and memorabilia organization

- Planning, packing, and unpacking for relocation
- Preparing medical insurance forms
- Rearranging living space
- Remodeling closets, garages, and storage spaces

This is just the short list; some organizers provide even more services. If you plan to take advantage of any professional organizing services, check at what rate they are billed. Hourly rates might vary based on the type of service.

## How much does a professional organizer cost?

Professional organizers charge a wide range of hourly fees, and they're usually based on the organizer's level of experience. Typically, you can expect to pay an organizer somewhere between $50 to $200 per hour, which may or may not include supplies needed to complete or the organizer's travel time. I suggest calling more than one organizer in your area to get a feel for the range of prices. Keep in mind, though, that it doesn't always pay to make your choice based on the hourly rate alone, This can be one of those situations in which you get what you pay for. For example, Organizer A might charge $80 an hour and include needed supplies. Organizer B might charge $50 an hour, charge $25 per appointment for travel expenses, require a minimum number of hours, require an advance to be paid at the first appointment, and charge extra for supplies. Have all the facts before you make your choice.

## What questions should I ask when interviewing an organizer?

Keep in mind that your relationship with a professional organizer will be a very personal one. He or she will be in your home and helping you go through your belongings. Because most organizers work on an hourly basis, you can decide how long you and your organizer work together. Be wary of any organizer who asks you to sign a long-term contract. Most professional organizers I know are nonjudgmental, encouraging, and supportive. Choose an organizer who is a good listener and flexible, and not one who will try to force solutions that won't work for you. Interview several professional organizers before choosing one. You might even prefer to meet the organizer in person before making a decision. Some organizers offer a free consultation, while others might charge for a consultation but then credit that fee if they are hired. Still others might charge a flat fee for an assessment and another fee for in-home, hands-on service. Here are some questions you should ask when interviewing professional organizers:

- What services do you provide?
- Do you have areas of specialization?
- Have you worked with situations like mine?
- How long have you been a professional organizer?
- What results can I expect from your service?
- How long is a typical work session?
- Can you estimate how long we'd need to work together?
- How accurate have your estimates been in the past?
- Who will I be working with?
- How do you charge for your services?
- Will you charge for travel?
- Do you require a contract? If so, what are the terms?
- Do you have references?
- Is the work of your company guaranteed?
- Is there a fee for the initial consultation?
- Do you have a confidentiality policy?
- What is your cancellation policy?

- Will you require "before" and "after" photos for your portfolio?
- Do you provide any supplies we may need? If so, is there an extra charge?
- What methods of payment do you accept?
- How and when is payment made?
- Do you offer any discount if we need multiple hours together?
- When you come over, will you tour my entire home and offer me a plan?
- Will you suggest between-session work for me to do on my own?
- Can you tell me how you plan to conduct our first appointment?
- Do you offer any type of follow-up?
- If we need help, like a handyman, do you have someone we can call?
- Are you able to customize your solutions to suit my needs?

A great organizer also will have questions for you, so be prepared to answer questions like:

- Does anyone else live in your home with you?
- What are you looking for?
- Why do you think your attempts haven't been successful?
- Have you ever worked with an organizer before?
- If so, what was the experience like?
- What prompted you to look for an organizer now?
- Do you have a deadline for the project?

## I'd like to hire a professional organizer, but what if I'm too embarrassed to let someone see my mess?

Ideally, after interviewing professional organizers, you'll choose one with whom you feel at ease. You also should feel secure in the knowledge that organizers have seen it all before. And although you may feel vulnerable about revealing your level of disorganization, it is often not nearly as bad as you think it is. Professional organizers are not judgmental people and truly enjoy helping someone take an area from chaotic to clear. If you're still uncomfortable with the thought of an organizer visiting your home, there are organizers who are willing to work with you over the phone. This is a very different situation than working together hands-on, but it can be as effective. You can find a listing of organizers at www.JamieNovak.com.

## Should I hire a professional organizer to help someone else who is disorganized?

Generally this is not a good idea, unless the other person has clearly expressed that she wants an organizer. If the person you're trying to help isn't on board with the idea of a professional organizer, your hiring one might insult her, and your efforts most likely will be wasted. Even if the person is agreeable to your hiring someone, it might not work out because the person really doesn't have anything invested in the process. If you know a person who wants to get more organized, a better solution might be to offer to babysit or give her a gift certificate for any products or furniture she might need to keep the space organized.

## Why hire a professional organizer?

Because some projects need professional help. If you're dreaming of something but not actually doing it, paying to have it done can be priceless. Professional organizers know what they're doing, so they eliminate the time-consuming trial and error of setting up ineffective systems. They also know which products work best to avoid costly mistakes.

Consider the amount of time you waste each day because you are disorganized. Sometimes the "born organized" people we know assume everyone has organizing skills, but that's simply not true.

Investing some time and money to learn how to organize can be the best thing you ever did. How stressed out are you? Are you having disagreements with family members? Are you passing down poor organizing habits to your children? How much money do you spend replacing things that you know you have but just can't find? How much do you spend on late fees because a bill was misplaced and paid after the due date, or because a movie was returned late? Spending a session or two with a professional organizer at $50 to $200 an hour can be a bargain compared to what you're spending now in time, stress, and money. Plus, leaving the work to a professional can save your time and your sanity.

# Chapter 3

## ORGANIZING 101

- What are organizing "leftovers," and how can I deal with them?
- Should I sell, give away, or just throw away the stuff I'm ready to part with?
- How can I locate a charity if I want to donate my items?
- What's my donation worth?
- Besides a charity, where can I donate stuff?
- I've heard that you can rent big-ticket items rather than buying them. Will this help me stay organized?
- How can I dispose of hazardous waste?
- What should be shredded instead of just thrown away?
- How can I stop wasting money by forgetting to return things or returning them without a receipt?
- What's the best way to organize and store all of my important papers?
- Am I the only one who can't have guests drop by because there is too much stuff to clean up?
- What is a "maybe box," and do I need one?
- Is a treasure box a good idea?
- What's the easiest way to organize my photographs?
- Is it acceptable to keep photos in boxes, or do I have to put them into albums?
- What is the best way to trim down and organize a collection?
- How can I create a household inventory?
- I bought lots of containers to organize things, but they're still empty. What should I do next?
- How can I stop taking home free stuff?
- Why doesn't my friend's way of organizing work for me?
- Where should I start when the clutter is so overwhelming, I think the only answer is a Dumpster?
- What if a family member needs organizing help but resists all my attempts to help?
- How can I locate and organize my aging parents' important belongings?
- What are some ideas for organizing family history, things like stories and genealogy?
- How can I move past the sorting step to the next step?

- Will labeling things help me stay organized?
- Do you recommend color-coding?
- When will my family member notice the clutter and clean up?
- How can I tell if an item is worth selling?
- How can I sell items online?
- Are some gadgets just more trouble than they're worth?
- How can I lighten the load of things I carry with me in my purse?
- How can I stop bringing unnecessary junk home from garage sales?
- How long do you recommend holding on to product boxes in case they are needed for returns?
- How do I begin cleaning and organizing my garage?
- I inherited boxes of family heirlooms. How do I find out if they're worth something?
- How can I organize my sewing and craft supplies?
- How can I avoid buying organization solutions that do not fit the space?

## What are organizing "leftovers," and how can I deal with them?

Leftovers are all those little items left over after you've completed your organizing project. Leftovers are things like a one-inch bit of crayon, a lens from a broken pair of sunglasses, or a charging cord from an outdated cell phone. Many leftover items are junk and simply can be thrown out or recycled, but you might not be ready to take that step. If you're a saver, it can take some time to feel okay about tossing the items. Once you do toss them, however, you'll feel a great sense of relief. If the items are truly items to keep, then they simply need a home. You could create a leftover box; simply place the items into a box and sort the box when it starts to overflow. The leftover box gives the items a home and gives you time to think about them. You'll still have the items should you need them (though you probably won't), and soon you'll be able to part with them.

## Should I sell, give away, or just throw away the stuff I'm ready to part with?

It depends. To avoid adding more unnecessary stuff to already-crowded landfills and to provide people in need with new or gently used items, I suggest donating everything you can to charity, or even to a friend or family member. Of course, there are always going to be items that simply need to be thrown away or recycled.

The prospect of selling can be a little tricky. The allure of posting an item on an online auction site and watching the bids skyrocket can be tempting. But first consider whether the item is valuable. Take a moment to search an online auction site to see who might be selling the same item and how much they are asking for it, and research www.ztail.com to easily see the current value of an item. Or, check a value guidebook in the reference section of your local library. Then consider whether you're gifted at writing a compelling ad for the item. You need to be computer literate to post the ad as well as a quality photo of the item. Keep in mind that you'll have to store the item until it is sold, take the time to ship the item, and collect your profit minus the listing and other miscellaneous fees. If the item is delivered to the buyer damaged or broken, you might have to spend time resolving a dispute. If this process sounds appealing, or if you enjoy running yard sales, then try selling. Alternatively you can take the items to an online auction store where the staff will do all the work for you. When the item sells, they'll take their commission and send you a check. You most likely will have to pay taxes if the item sells.

## How can I locate a charity if I want to donate my items?

Finding a local charity is as easy as opening your phone directory or searching online—just look for thrift stores. Many charities operate stores where they sell donated items and use the money to support their cause. You also can scan your town's newspaper. Often, thrift stores place small ads or write-ups about special charitable drives. Here are some additional charities to consider:

- Book Project, www.internationalbookproject.org
- Call to Protect, www.calltoprotect.org
- Call to Recycle, www.calltorecycle.org
- City Links, www.citylinks.org
- Computers 4 Kids, www.c4k.org
- Computers for Schools, www.pcsforschools.org
- Darien Book Aid, www.dba.darien.org
- DonateMyDress.org
- Donation Center, www.geappliances.com
- Excess Quantities, www.excessaccess.com
- Furniture Bank Association, www.thenfba.org or www.help1up.org
- Gift of Sight, www.givethegiftofsight.com or www.giftsforsight.org
- Glass Slipper Project, www.glassslipperproject.org
- Global Literacy Project, www.glpinc.org
- Goodwill, www.goodwill.org
- Half Price Books, www.halfpricebooks.com
- The Humane Society of the United States, www.hsus.org/furdonation
- Hungry for Music, www.hungryformusic.org
- In Kind, www.inkindex.com
- International Book Project, www.intlbookproject.org
- National Cristina Foundation, www.cristina.org
- New Eyes for the Needy, www.neweyesfortheneedy.org
- On It Foundation, www.TheOnItFoundation.org
- One Warm Coat, www.onewarmcoat.org

- Operation Happy Note, www.operationhappynote.com
- Police Athletic League, www.nationalpal.org
- Prison Reader, www.prisonreader.org
- Re-use a Shoe, www.letmeplay.com
- Reader to Reader, www.readertoreader.org
- Red Cross, www.redcross.org
- Salvation Army, www.salvationarmy.com
- World Computer Exchange, www.worldcomputerexchange.org

Jot down the phone numbers for these charities and post them near your phone. The list will be a visual reminder to find more stuff to give away, and save you time looking up the contact information. Remember that most charities are staffed by volunteers who might get overwhelmed by a carload of donations. Most prefer frequent small donations, so don't wait—call them even if you only have a bag or two to donate.

## What's my donation worth?

The Internal Revenue Service (IRS) accepts the estimates from the Salvations Army's valuation guide, available online at www.satruck.org/ValueGuide.aspx. You can use this data to calculate the monetary value of your charitable donations and claim the deduction on your tax return. It is highly recommended that you get and keep a receipt showing the date and amount of the donation. It is also a good idea to have an itemized list. Most charities do not provide this list for you, so as you pack the items, keep a running tally and description of them. Include the type, size, material, date purchased, amount paid, and whether the item is new or used. For example, you might write "0 to 3-month girl shirt, new with tags, price $7.95." Note that the amount you paid for the item is not the amount of the tax deduction. The amount of the deduction is based on the estimate of the item's current value. A charitable resale shop will not be able to sell that shirt for $7.95; it may price the shirt at $3.00, and that is the value for tax purposes.

## Besides a charity, where can I donate stuff?

Many local churches, synagogues, homeless shelters, schools, senior centers, and theater companies accept donations. They may want old clothing, small furniture, old artwork, books, CDs, videos, computers, furniture, rugs, or kitchenware. An earth-friendly option is to swap your belongings. You do not always need to take an item in exchange; you can simply give. Visit these websites for more information:

- www.Allrecipes.com
- www.Couponlist.com
- www.CraigsList.com
- www.ExcessAccess.com
- www.FreeCycle.org
- www.FreeUse.org
- www.Frugalreader.com
- www.GardenWeb.com
- www.Homeexchangevacation.com
- www.Homelink.org
- www.Makeupalley.com
- www.Paperbackswap.com
- www.Swaphandmedowns.com
- www.SwapStyle.com
- www.swapthing.com
- www.swaptreasures.com
- www.titletrader.com
- www.zunafish.com

## I've heard that you can rent big-ticket items rather than buying them. Will this help me stay organized?

Yes. Instead of buying something you'll only use once, consider renting and returning an item so it doesn't become clutter. Imagine getting your hands on a dress from a high-end designer, a necklace that costs more than your car, or a handbag that is on waitlist for VIPs. You can do just that at places like www.OneNightAffair.com, www.BagBorrowSteal.com, and www.BorrowedBling.com. Simply log on and "shop" for an item you want to borrow. Check out, and the item is shipped to you. Enjoy it for as long as you like. When you're ready to ship it back, use the preprinted shipping label. Borrowing rates for designer wedding dresses, for example, start at just $65, and you can borrow a fancy cocktail ring for just $10. Before agreeing to anything, first read the fine print on the website or call the company directly. It may be worth it to spend a few extra dollars on any insurance the company offers in the event something happens to the item.

## How can I dispose of hazardous waste?

Visit www.earth911.org and enter your zip code to get a list of local drop-off centers for hazardous waste or seasonal waste like Christmas trees.

You can also check out:

- www.LooseFillPackaging.com, for places to get rid of packing material
- www.RedJellyFish.org, for places to donate old cell phones
- www.RecycledGoods.com, for places to donate an old computer

Another option is to check with your municipal building. Many towns offer yearly hazardous waste pickup or a one-time bulk pickup at no charge.

## What should be shredded instead of just thrown away?

Shred anything that contains your name, address, or other sensitive data, including invoices, receipts, statements, personalized pitch letters and envelopes, catalogs, and preapproved credit offers. Identity thieves find these key pieces of information most useful: your name, address, phone number, date of birth, Social Security number, driver's license number, credit card information, bank account information, and your mother's maiden name. Get a cross-cut shredder. Older shredders simply cut in strips that can be pieced back together by a patient thief. Place the shredder near the spot where you sort your mail. That way, you can shred quickly instead of making a pile to be shredded later. A shredder that accommodates up to twelve or more sheets of paper at one pass and also allows for credit cards, staples, and paper clips will significantly reduce the amount of time you spend shredding and prevent annoying jams. If you can't purchase your own shredder, take your paper and other items to a shredding event. A mobile shredding company called Shred It hosts free, on-the-spot shredding for as many papers as you can carry. The company shreds the pile right in front of you, and it only takes about three seconds to shred a large box of papers. You can find more information about local events at www.ShredIt.com or by calling 1-800-697-4733.

## How can I stop wasting money by forgetting to return things or returning them without a receipt?

Returning purchases is one of the most expensive consequences of disorganization. One way to cut back on the number of returns to be made is to be very thoughtful about purchases. If you're not sure about buying something, don't just buy it anyway. Forgo the purchase and think about it more before you make a bad decision. If you practice this method, you'll have fewer items to return. For the purchases you do make, keep a single envelope in your purse or wallet to collect all the item receipts.

## What's the best way to organize and store all of my important papers?

Try something I call the "no-fail binder solution." Use a simple three-ring binder to store information on a similar topic. Here's how to create your own:

1.  Decide on the type of binder you're going to create (see the list of suggested topics below).
2.  Inside the binder, insert three-hole-punched notebook paper (for jotting down ideas), clear plastic page protectors to hold important papers, a zippered pouch to hold pens or loose, items and tabbed dividers to categorize the binder.
3.  Label the spine of the binder and start using it.

Here are some of the most common topics for organizing important papers:

- **Association:** paperwork relating to the organization or group you belong to
- **Bill payment:** creditors, envelopes, stamps, calculator, checkbook
- **Business cards:** contacts, business cards, and return addresses from envelopes
- **Driving directions:** printed from the computer, maps, handwritten directions

- **Entertainment and recreation:** movies to see, books to read, places to visit, and other lists
- **Family members:** a binder for each family member, with items like schedules and addresses
- **Financial:** information on your financial accounts
- **Fitness information:** clippings and ideas for getting fit, stored by category
- **Gardening:** plant care tags, lists of what you planted and their success rates
- **Greeting cards:** greeting cards sectioned by category
- **Hobby instructions:** directions and ideas for your hobby
- **Household manual:** important contacts, play date telephone numbers, class schedules
- **Job search:** résumés, list of contacts, employment opportunities
- **Medical records:** physicians' names, copies of reports, medications list
- **Moving:** utility contact information, mover estimates, to-do lists
- **New baby:** hospital information, baby name ideas, doctor information
- **Party:** location ideas, menu, guest lists, business cards
- **Recipes:** clipped recipes sectioned by category
- **Reference clippings:** clippings of interest from magazines and newspapers
- **Remodeling:** paint swatches, business cards, estimates, fabric swatches
- **School papers:** children's retuned tests, half-done homework, and so on
- **Take-out menus:** restaurant take-out menus (keep duplicates in your car)
- **To read:** items you've been meaning to read so you can take them with you

- **Travel ideas:** ideas, plans, brochures, prices, travel agencies, websites
- **Vacation:** what you want to see, packing lists, itinerary
- **Warranties and manuals:** warranties, receipts, and manuals stored by category
- **Wedding:** planning, ideas, contracts, business cards, guest lists

**Note:** if you plan to have more than one category per binder, use tabs to separate the topics. Once your binders are ready, you can store the commonly referenced ones on a bookshelf or in a kitchen cabinet. Others can be stored where they will be used, for example, the garden one in the garage, the recipes one in the kitchen.

## Am I the only one who can't have guests drop by because there is too much stuff to clean up?

Not at all. In fact, the results of an informal poll on my website reveal that more than 82 percent of people are embarrassed to let others see at least one room in their home. More than half have homes with clutter on at least one-third of the horizontal spaces (tables, countertops, sofas, and floors). Although clutter is more common than you might imagine, that does not make it any less stressful. The good news is that you can take control and do something about it so you can live without the fear of having friends and family drop by. Some of the most organized people you know have a secret: They're just better at disguising the clutter than you are. Clean does not always mean organized.

## What is a "maybe box," and do I need one?

It depends. If you have trouble parting with items, a maybe box may be just the answer. A maybe box is designed to be a temporary safety net in case you change your mind about letting go of something. Fill a cardboard box with items that maybe you'll use, but maybe you won't. These might include toys your child outgrew but might ask for in the next few months, or stacks of cooking magazines you might read if you find the time. Make a list of the contents on the outside of the box, tape the box shut, write an expiration date on the outside of the box (six to twelve months is a good time period), and store it. If you need anything from the box before the expiration date, you can easily get it from the box. However, if you do not use the items by the expiration, donate them to charity or discard the entire box without looking inside. If you look inside, you'll most likely become reattached to the items and unable to let them go. Chances are, once you make a maybe box or two and never need anything from it, you'll find that you no longer need the boxes at all. You'll feel much more confident in your decisions as to what to keep and what to discard.

## Is a treasure box a good idea?

Treasure boxes are a great idea. They are the perfect way to store sentimental items and other treasures. You and each member of your family should have a box to keep all your special items. Write the person's name on the outside of the box and store it in a closet or other place where it is easily accessible in case you want to add items. If the treasure box isn't accessible, items that should go inside will end up as clutter. If an item is too large to fit in the box, simply take a photo of it, let the item go, and store the photo in your treasure box.

## What's the easiest way to organize my photographs?

First, gather all the photos you can without too much trouble— don't scour the attic for boxes and bags of photos. Start with the photos that are handy and incorporate the others into the new system as you find them. This also means you'll eventually need to develop any undeveloped rolls of film, including disposable cameras.

Once you have the photos, sort them by event, person, or chronologically. While sorting, have a few envelopes with you so you can put aside photos to send to other people. If you have kids, you might want to make a box of photos they can use for school projects. If you have duplicates, keep one and share the other with friends or family, or recycle it. Don't feel you have to hold on to photos you don't like. Sorting the photos will take some time, and it will take even more time if you get sidetracked by reminiscing as you sort them. Take your time and work in small increments instead of marathon sessions that can wear you out and cause you to lose your motivation. Sort photos while you watch television, or make it a family affair by hosting a photo-organizing party. Invite family members over to help you and share the memories, or ask them to bring their own photos and you can all sort together.

Once you've sorted the photos, the next step is to store them. Precious photos like those of your wedding day or a new baby should be placed in a disaster-proof box for safekeeping. This is also where you should store important negatives. Use acid-free photo-safe boxes and store them away from direct sunlight, extreme temperatures, and moisture. Standard photo-safe boxes fit about one thousand photos and include tabbed dividers.

## Is it acceptable to keep photos in boxes, or do I have to put them into albums?

My philosophy is to go with whatever works for you. Photos can be enjoyed and shared from a photo-safe box just as easily as from a photo album. If you choose to put your photos into albums, be sure to clearly label the spines. That way, you can find the photos you want without searching through all of your photo albums. You might even choose to leave most of your photos in boxes while creating a few special themed albums, focusing on a vacation or other special event, for example.

Whatever is easiest for you—boxes or albums—is the system you should choose. If the system isn't easy, you won't use it.

## What is the best way to trim down and organize a collection?

Unchecked collections can quickly overrun your home. Limiting the amount of space you allocate to store the collection is the best way to keep collections at a manageable size. If you only allow one shelf of a bookcase to be used for your magazine collection, then you can only keep as many as fit there.

This method uses what I call a "par level." A par level is a predetermined amount of a specific item you want to store. Using par levels eliminates the debate about what to buy and keep. For example, if a single shelf in your pantry is allocated for paper towels and you know that eight rolls fit there, then eight rolls of paper towel becomes your par level. If you come across a sale on paper towels and know you have eight rolls at home, then you don't have to decide whether or not to buy more. Par levels also can help control clutter in a bigger way. Knowing how much space you have for items and that you need to leave room for more stuff to come, you know how much you can store. Problems arise when your stuff outgrows the space you've allocated for it. Therefore, setting par levels for collections can spell success.

## How can I create a household inventory?

A household inventory is a complete catalog of all the personal property located in your home and elsewhere, like garages or storage facilities. If you don't have a current inventory, make one in the next month. Once the inventory is complete, update it each time you change your clocks for daylight saving time. That way, you only need to remember about six months of new purchases or items you discarded. A perfect time to create an inventory is when you're packing up to move to a new home. Even if you're not moving, don't put off taking inventory. Creating a list of household items in advance is much easier than trying to remember all of your belongings after property is stolen or destroyed. Here are some tips for creating a household inventory:

- Record the location of the originals of all important financial and family documents, such as birth and marriage certificates, wills, deeds, tax returns, insurance policies, and stock and bond certificates. Keep the originals in a safe place and store copies elsewhere. You'll need accessible records for tax and insurance purposes.
- Go from room to room using a camera and/or video camera to make a record of your possessions. Write notes describing each item, when you bought it, how much it cost, and any special features or characteristics like "solid oak kitchen cabinets" versus just "kitchen cabinets." Be sure to include model and serial numbers. To get the value of an item in seconds, go to www.ztail.com.
- Don't overlook less expensive items, such as bath towels and clothes. Their costs add up if you have to replace them.
- Make copies of receipts and canceled checks for more valuable items.
- Get professional appraisals of jewelry, collectibles, artwork, or other items that are difficult to value.
- Be sure you include the items in your attic, basement, and garage or stored off-site in a storage facility or at a family member's home.
- Remember to photograph cars, boats, and recreational vehicles.

Most importantly, once you've completed your inventory, leave a copy with relatives or friends, or in a safe deposit box. Don't leave your only copy at home, where it might be destroyed along with your possessions in the event of a disaster. To make creating your household inventory a breeze, try budget-friendly computer software programs, like Collectify, designed for this purpose. This type of software makes the task much easier by allowing you to simply fill in the blanks and save photos.

## I bought lots of containers to organize things, but they're still empty. What should I do next?

Sounds like you had some good intentions, but you didn't know exactly what to do. When we don't know what to do, we usually do nothing, which is probably what happened in this case. Containers alone do not make us more organized—taking action does. The great news is that you already have the containers, so you're all set to go. The next step is to sort. Start with a single area or pile of stuff and work in short blocks of time, grouping similar items. Once you know what you have, you can place it in the containers. Be sure to clearly label the containers so you can easily identify what they contain. Labeling also makes it a snap to put items back in the right container.

## How can I stop taking home free stuff?

The lure of free stuff can be powerful. Some people can pass up freebies, but many simply can't walk away, and that's exactly what marketers are counting on. The real question is, "Is it really free?" For example, if you buy a new brand of shampoo just to get the free conditioner but never use the shampoo, was the conditioner really free? Or, if you grab a few promotional pens from the bank kiosk and dump them in your junk drawer at home, but then waste time looking for items in the cluttered junk drawer, was the pen really free? I don't think so; your time is worth a great deal. To break yourself of the freebie habit, ask yourself: "Do I really need this?" and "Where am I going to put this?" If you answered yes to the first question and have an answer for the second one, take the free items home. Before you bring them into your home, ask yourself the same questions again. If your answers haven't change, bring the items inside. In most cases, the second time you answer the questions, you'll catch yourself and leave the item behind.

## Why doesn't my friend's way of organizing work for me?

Everyone has their own style, way of doing things, likes, and personality, so there are no cookie-cutter solutions. What works for one person may never work for another, so try not to compare someone else's methods to your own. Many times a spin-off solution works well, but you have to try it first to find out. You may like things to be out on shelves while someone else may prefer them to be behind closed doors. No solution is right or wrong. If it works for you, then run with it.

## Where should I start when the clutter is so overwhelming, I think the only answer is a Dumpster?

It might make you laugh to think the only answer is a Dumpster, but you might be laughing only so you don't cry. When a mess is so extreme that every household surface is covered and there is little room to move throughout the home, it is an overwhelming prospect to even think about where to begin. In addition to that type of clutter, you probably have other issues to deal with, including a lack of energy, doing anything to avoid being home, an inability to part with items (separation anxiety), or physical limitations. The clutter in your home might be out of hand due to reasons beyond your control like an illness, surgery, death of a loved one, loss of a job, or other cause.

The great news is that no matter how bad you think things are, you can get organized. The best place to start is in the heart of the home, the kitchen. Once your kitchen is organized, it is much easier to tackle the adjoining rooms. The first order of business in the kitchen is to clear the visible surfaces like the countertops and table. Grab a notepaper, pen, and some boxes or laundry baskets to sort items into as you clear them. Place papers in one container and rarely used small appliances in another. As you clear the surfaces, you'll find items to toss, recycle, or donate. Once the surfaces are cleared, you'll have plenty of surface space to use as you finish organizing the kitchen and move on to other rooms.

## What if a family member needs organizing help but resists all my attempts to help?

The simple fact is that nobody, not even you, can make someone else get organized. In fact, attempting to force someone to organize or doing it for him or her only makes the situation worse. Imagine how you would feel if someone came in with a big black bag and started collecting your beloved items to take out to the garbage. Although you may think your family member's items are trash and, yes, in some cases they truly are, they are meaningful to the person who owns them. You may not think someone needs a certain item, but that is not your decision to make.

Concentrate on organizing all of your belongings and, if necessary, come to a compromise with your family member about how much space his stuff can take up and where he can and can not pile it. Leading by example can inspire your family member to organize his or her own belongings. Encouragement and support go a long way; nagging and threats will stunt any progress.

## How can I locate and organize my aging parents' important belongings?

It can be difficult for older people who have collected items throughout a lifetime to abruptly change their ways. Express your concerns and offer to work with your parents a few hours a week to make headway in organizing their things. One way to approach the topic is to say that you know there are family items meant to be passed down, and that by going through them now you can record their history before the stories are lost. Whether or not you are able to help your parents organize their belongings, it is imperative that you know where to find all of the important documents. A conversation about final arrangements can be extremely difficult, but it is a necessary part of life. Going about it in an organized fashion can help make it easier. Here's a list of your parents' important documents that you need to locate:

- Insurance: Medicare/Medicaid number, supplement, other policies
- Physicians: names, phone numbers, and other contact information
- Medical history: medications, allergies, conditions, procedures
- Identification: Social Security card, military ID, driver's license number
- Address list: friends, neighbors, family
- Service providers: attorney, financial advisor, clergy, accountant
- Financial: account numbers, checkbook, investments, tax records
- Legal: wills, powers of attorney, health care directives
- Deeds: house, other property, car title, boat title

- Insurance: life, medical, auto, home
- Household: mortgage, apartment lease, property tax records
- Vital records: birth certificate, marriage license, divorce decree
- Final wishes: organ donation, burial, property distribution

## What are some ideas for organizing family history, things like stories and genealogy?

These are time-sensitive items, because some family history might be lost if members of your family are not able to share it before they are gone. Losing a family member is not a happy topic to consider, but not having a record of their story after they're gone is even more painful. There are a variety of ways to lose family history; death is of course one way, but a person's memory can fail, records that are not backed up can be lost or destroyed, or family disagreements can cause a breakdown in communication, including the sharing of family history. So we need to gather it, organize it, and protect it for generations to come.

There are many ways to capture family history, depending on how computer savvy you and your family are. You can always collect and make copies of heirloom photos, or you can scan them into your computer and save them to a CD. You also can create a family website, using one of many no-cost Internet hosting options available. Documents also can be scanned and saved, and the actual paper version stored in a waterproof, disaster-proof box. Collecting and organizing family stories is relatively easy via email. Try sending periodic questions to family members, who can then write back to share a story, a fun family fact, or other goodie. For family members who aren't comfortable using email, simply print your message and mail it to them. Family videos and video clips also can be captured and burned onto DVD. Remember to locate as many family letters as you can find, such as letters between your grandmother and grandfather. Scan them into an electronic file and store the originals in photo-safe boxes to prevent damage.

## How can I move past the sorting step to the next step?

Sorting might seem less intimidating than actually deciding what to keep, what to toss, and what to put away. It's no wonder, then, that people get stuck in sorting mode. You might sort a pile of papers into categories and spread each of those piles across the dining room table. When you need to use the table, however, you probably pile up the sorted, and the sorting has to start again. Think of how accomplished you'll feel to sort and then put away. Remember, you can always go back later and change how you've put away something; the goal is simply to put things away so you can move on.

## Will labeling things help me stay organized?

Yes, you should try to label, within reason. It can be addicting, so refrain from labeling everything that stands still long enough. Most people think labeling is useful because it helps them find things, but labeling also helps you and your family members see where to put things away. If a container is labeled, you'll likely to think twice before tossing something where it does not belong. It takes a little time to label things, but it will save you time in the long run. For example, if you label your pantry with general categories it will only take a glance to see what's missing when planning your grocery shopping list.

## Do you recommend color-coding?

Sometimes. Most people are very visual, and it is quicker and easier to spot a color than read a word. So color-coding can work well for lots of things. The key is to not get carried away by choosing too many colors. That can make it difficult to remember what each color means. Color-coding can be helpful to differentiate personal file folders from business file folders, for example. Color-coding your children's belongings also works well; the blue bag belongs to one child while the red belongs to another. Color-coding doesn't work so well when you run out of a certain color. For example, you might use orange organizing tubs to store fall decorations, but when you run out of space and need to buy another tub for fall decorations, you can't find an orange one. You decide to buy a green one instead. Now you have some fall decorations in orange tubs and some in a green tub, which throws off your color-coding scheme. In lieu of coding with words or colors, pictures are a good option. A picture of dolls can go on the playroom bin where the dolls belong. A picture of a snowflake can go on the boxes for winter decorations.

## When will my family member notice the clutter and clean up?

Instead of waiting for someone to notice, try being proactive. Present that person with a specific request. Ask something like, "Would you please pick up your shoes from the floor and put them in the shoe cabinet, and put your cereal bowl in the dishwasher before you leave for work?" If you have a deadline for the task, state it. You also can assign a level of importance to the task, like, "This is a ten on a level of one to ten."

## How can I tell if an item is worth selling?

Most of us have wondered if an item tucked away in a closet or attic could possibly be worth a bunch of money. We've all heard stories about someone who had a knickknack they were going to toss only to discover it was worth an obscene amount of money. Sure it would be nice, but what are the chances? To find out whether your item is a goldmine, follow these steps:

1.  Choose an item from the pile of possible treasures.
2.  Log on to an online auction site where others are selling items like yours and search for the item you own. You can search a variety of ways, including by keywords, titles, or identifying marks. Once you've tracked down the item, see who else has one and how much they are selling it for. You can do more research at the library, using reference books like *The Collectibles Price Guide*, or you can visit www.ztail.com. If you need more expert help, locate a certified appraiser through websites such as www.appraisers.org. Appraisers can offer you an unbiased opinion.
3.  Once you know what the item is truly worth, you can decide what to do with it: keep and use it, toss it, recycle it, donate it, or sell it.

To give you an idea of the worth of certain items, here's a sample of recent online sales:

*   Vintage (more than thirty years old) Fisher-Price toys: $475 each
*   Well-known board games: $19 each
*   Queen-size mattress (new with tags): $450
*   1953 *TV Guide* with Bob Hope and Queen Elizabeth on the cover: $5.00
*   Mint condition Hummel figurine #471: $350
*   1971 *National Geographic:* $2.00

## How can I sell items online?

Gather the items for sale and place them in a safe spot. Then complete the following steps:

1. Write a detailed description of the item. Use catchy words and phrases to market the item well.
2. Take great photos of the item. First make sure the item is clean by wiping off dirt, smudges, and fingerprints. If the item is plastic, shine it with cleaning wipes. Note: do not try to clean known antiques since that most likely will lessen the value. Set the stage by positioning the item so its good features are highlighted. For example, if the tag is still on a garment, get a close-up of the tag. If the item is an article of clothing, hang it from a hanger instead of simply placing it on a flat surface.
3. Create a new email account to use just for these sales. That way, the messages won't clutter your everyday inbox.
4. Go to the website where you plan to sell the item and list it.
5. Wait for it to sell.
6. Pack it up, ship it off, and collect your money.

## Are some gadgets just more trouble than they're worth?

Absolutely. Many gadgets come with lots of pieces and take more time to clean than they do to use. Plus, you have to remember that you have them, be able to find them when you need them, and store them when they are not in use. Some gadgets are worthwhile. For example, I love my avocado slicer. But if you don't eat many avocados or you already have a great way to slice them, then you don't need the gadget. Choose your gadgets wisely, and ruthlessly weed out the ones you don't use.

## How can I lighten the load of things I carry with me in my purse?

First, contain similar items in makeup cases or small bags inside your purse (snack-size ziplock bags save time because you can see what's inside at a glance). Put gums and mints in one bag, pens and notepaper in another. Now you can easily leave behind the bags that you won't need for an outing. Choose a bright-colored wallet or a bag with a contrasting lining so you can find things easily—a black wallet inside a purse that has a black lining can be difficult to find. Whenever possible, leave less frequently used items in your car's glove box. Then consider how much you are actually carrying with you. Unless there is a gum emergency, you don't need three packs; leave some at home. If you haven't used your mini sewing kit in years, don't take it with you.

### How can I stop bringing unnecessary junk home from garage sales?

If buying junk from garage sales has become part of your weekend routine, try changing your routine. If you run errands on Saturday mornings when the garage sales start, try running errands another time during the week and stay home during peak garage sale times. If you just can't stay away from garage sales, go, but take a limited amount of cash and bring a list of only a few treasures you want. That way, the garage sale will be more of a treasure hunt than a shopping spree.

### How long do you recommend holding on to product boxes in case they are needed for returns?

It depends on the item. Most items have a ninety-day or shorter return policy and up to a one-year manufacturer's warranty. To be on the safe side, keep the box for this period for a hassle-free return. The easiest way to store the box is to break it down so it is flat, then write an expiration date on the box, most likely ninety days to a year from the purchase date (check your receipt). Try to keep all the boxes in the same place, so if you need to tape one back together for a return you know just where it is. Good storage places for boxes are under a bed, in the garage, beside a refrigerator, or on one side of a closet. If you're really short on space, push your couch against the wall and slide the boxes between the wall and the couch. Try to keep toy boxes until you're sure your child likes the toy and it is in good working order. Also hold on to computer and electronics boxes, software and video game boxes, and small appliance boxes.

## How do I begin cleaning and organizing my garage?

Many people use their garage for temporary storage of items, but somehow the items end up staying there. The garage is a versatile storage space, housing anything from cars to gardening supplies to high school memories. It's no wonder, then, that many garages become a chaotic mix of stuff, making it impossible to find what you need. Here are ten steps to follow to clean out your garage and transform it into a useful space:

1. Sort your stuff. First, determine what's in your garage. Start by sorting everything into categories. Separate the gardening supplies from the car maintenance supplies from the sporting equipment and so on. This "like with like" principle is a basic, yet powerful, organizing technique.
2. Toss the trash. Keep a few heavy-duty garbage bags on hand as you sort items and toss the trash. Be ruthless—toss broken equipment, rusted tools, and toys that are missing pieces. Dispose of any long overdue recycling piles and check www. earth911.org for hazardous waste drop-off locations for things like computer equipment and old antifreeze. Home supply stores sell a powder mix that can be added to cans of paint, making them safe to throw away.

3.  Share your stuff. Once you've separated your items into like groups and tossed the trash, you might be surprised to see how much good stuff you own. Keep only the best and give away the rest.

    • Give away unused items for free at www.freecycle.org
    • Give borrowed items to their rightful owner
    • Schedule a garage sale for the items you've earmarked
    • Give back abandoned family items

4.  Measure the space. To see exactly how much room you have for storage, park your car(s) in the garage with the doors and trunk open. Use chalk to outline the space they take up on the floor. Measure the gap from the top of the open trunk to the ceiling; you can then hang bikes or skis knowing your car will still fit.

5.  Designate the space. The items you keep need a home, and the garage floor is not an option. Designate the space, breaking it up into areas for specific items. Look at your item categories and pick an area of the garage for each to live. Keep accessibility in mind.

6.  Store it where you use it. Keep the items you use most in convenient locations. If you'll be storing your bulk paper goods in the garage, keep them nearest the door to the house. That way, you won't have to walk through the entire garage for a roll of paper towels. Store infrequently used items in places that are harder to reach, like the rafters.

7.  Add storage options. Now is the time to add shelving and cabinets, and to buy tubs and bins. Old kitchen cabinets hung on the wall can add valuable storage space. Use all the space from the floor to the ceiling. Hang what you can

from the walls and the ceiling. Be creative; use the backs of doors and the insides of cabinet doors for added storage. Try www.flowwall.com for creative storage ideas.

8. Give everything a home. Don't mix categories—when storing items, place similar items together. Leave room for additional items, as you'll probably get more. Use smaller containers that are easier to move when full. Protect treasured items in waterproof containers, and don't store photographs or other temperature- and moisture-sensitive items in the garage.

9. Label, label, label. Label each bin, shelf, container, and cabinet door. Labels make it much easier to put things away in the right spot. Label all sides of a container and the lid so you can read the contents from any direction.

10. Maintain the new system. Once you're done, reward yourself for all your hard work. To keep your garage looking great, break the old habits that caused the clutter in the first place. Adopt a household rule that you'll always put away an item when you're done with it.

These ten steps can help you say good-bye to garage clutter, but they only work if you take action. Dreaming about an organized garage isn't enough. The best way to transform your garage from chaotic to contained is to give yourself a deadline and get started. Work on small sections over a period of time, or hold a weekend marathon session. Organizing a garage is easier than you might think.

## I inherited boxes of family heirlooms. How do I find out if they're worth something?

Everyone dreams of finding that one inconspicuous item that ends up being worth a million dollars. To find out if you have such a treasure, you need to do a little homework or pay someone to do the research for you. When choosing an appraiser, you want an unbiased opinion, so the person who appraises the item should not be the same person who would buy it. Check the National Society of Appraisers for a local appraiser to provide advice. You also can research the item in question online at online auction sites. Find out how many people are selling similar items and for how much. Or you can visit www.ztail.com. The research librarians at your local library have access to a wealth of information and can direct you to valuation books that have information about specific items. Finally, try searching online for antique appraisals in your area. You might be pleasantly surprised to find that a local organization is hosting its own road show where you can have items assessed at no charge.

## How can I organize my sewing and craft supplies?

Try using bookcases for storage. Get plastic storage boxes and label them according to their contents, keeping similar items together. Hatboxes make great storage boxes and are attractive if you need to leave them out in the open on a bookcase shelf. You can store sewing or craft magazines and books on the bookcase shelf. Slide patterns into one-quart ziplock plastic bags and organize them according to type, for example, home decor, dresses, etc. Then place the bagged patterns in baskets on the shelves. Store thread in plastic containers with snap-on lids according to color so you can easily find the shade you need. Or check your local fabric store for a spool rack that you can hang on the wall to display spools of thread. A rolling cart with a flat top and drawers provides convenient, portable storage beside the sewing machine. Keep seam rippers, markers, beeswax, rulers, small scissors, and other supplies, in a box near the sewing machine. Place special buttons in ice cube trays that store easily in a drawer. Use a permanent market to write "sewing" on your sewing scissors so they don't get mixed up with other pairs of scissors in your home. A bulletin board can be a nice addition to any sewing space. Use it to display pattern ideas or fabric swatches, and as a place to keep measurements for family members or shopping lists. Hang measuring tapes from a straight pin stuck in the bulletin board.

If you would prefer to camouflage the sewing corner, use a three-paneled screen. Cabinets are also great for hiding notions and storage bins. Install as many as possible, because they'll help you use the otherwise wasted space. If you don't have the option of putting everything away, try blending the sewing items into your decor. Decorative baskets hide items attractively, and glass bottles look nice when filled with buttons, snaps, or other closures. Organize fabrics by hanging them on hangers according to color. Also, ask the staff at the fabric store for empty cardboard tubes from fabrics to store velvet, tapestry, or faux fur without permanently creasing them. Lastly, you might opt for an organizer from the hardware store. These offer anywhere from fifteen to 150 small drawers meant for screws and such. They work perfectly for beads and buttons and even lace. Hot glue a sample of what is inside to the outside of the drawer, so you can see what you have at a glance.

## How can I avoid buying organization solutions that do not fit the space?

The best answer is to measure your space before buying any organizing supplies. Then write down the measurements and bring them and a tape measure with you when you go to the store. To ensure you'll have a tape measure with you, put one in your purse or your car now. Then designate a small spiral notebook as your organizing notebook, where you'll write all your measurements and notes about what you need to buy. Whenever you need to buy items, make a list and note the size requirements. That way, you'll be much less likely to buy something that doesn't fit the space.

# Chapter 4

# EVERYDAY STUFF

- Where should I store gift wrap?
- How can I organize makeup samples and other free gifts?
- My car is a disaster zone. How can I keep it clean?
- How can I organize my wardrobe closet?
- My bathroom medicine cabinet is a big, jumbled mess. How can I make smaller items more accessible?
- What are some suggestions for storing pet items?
- How can I disguise the cables for all the electronics we charge every day?
- How can I organize my recycling?

## Where should I store gift wrap?

All gift-wrapping supplies, including bows and ribbon, are best stored together, usually under a bed. Bed risers can be used to lift the bed from the floor and provide additional storage space. An under-the-bed gift-wrapping container or some other shallow container is the best option for storing items. To avoid tearing the edges of rolls of wrap or having them unravel on you, slide them into the cut-off leg of a pair of pantyhose. Be sure to include a pair of scissors and some tape in the container so you'll have everything you need to wrap gifts in one place. Nest gift bags inside one another and slide them under the bed or stand them upright in a closet. Keep only a few generic gift bags in a variety of sizes; bags for specific occasions like a child's first birthday or a wedding tend to go to waste.

## How can I organize makeup samples and other free gifts?

First, determine whether you need to bring the items home. Free makeup samples can be tempting, but if they aren't your shade, brand, or style then consider leaving them behind. If you already have samples at home, keep them front and center or they'll be relegated to the back of a drawer or the bottom of a basket, never to be seen again. Use a basket to store all of your samples. Place it on the bathroom vanity so you can try a sample when you need something. After trying a sample, either keep it and use it or let it go. Consider donating unwanted samples to homeless or domestic violence shelters, or to the makeup department of the local community theater.

## My car is a disaster zone. How can I keep it clean?

These days, our vehicles can double as an office, restaurant, toy room, or movie theater. Front seats and floors are cluttered, CDs and DVDs have gone missing, and the trunk is packed with last year's sporting equipment. Here's my step-by-step plan for cleaning a vehicle and keeping it tidy:

1. Keep cleaning wipes and paper towels in the car for easy cleanup. Most wet messes are easier to clean before they dry.
2. Place one or two plastic bags in your car to collect trash. You can even put the bags in small garbage bins and secure them with Velcro to keep them handy. When the garbage is full, simply grab an extra plastic shopping bag next time you go grocery shopping, discard the bag of garbage from your car, and replace it with the empty bag.
3. Use over-the-seat organizers to keep children's toys, media items, cords, maps, umbrellas, gloves, and other essentials at hand.
4. Use milk crates, boxes, or cargo organizers to keep your trunk's contents organized. These work especially well to keep bags of groceries from tipping over.
5. Add organizing and washing your car to your house cleaning routine. Once a month, have a set appointment to organize the car.
6. Instead of allowing a few emergency items to roll around in your trunk, organize the space by making a roadside emergency kit. Put the following items in a duffel bag: spare warm clothing and comfortable shoes in case you need to keep warm or walk a distance; battery-powered radio and extra batteries; flashlight and extra batteries; blanket; booster cables; fire extinguisher (five-pound A-B-C type); first-aid kit and manual; bottled water; nonperishable high-energy foods, such as granola bars, raisins, and peanut butter; shovel; tire repair kit and pump; and flares. With all the items in one spot, you'll be able to find exactly what you need in the event of an emergency.

7. Put items for a small first-aid kit in your glove box so you can find what you need when you need it.
8. Make a new household rule that all family members are responsible for removing what they bring into the car. You might try "junk jail" for anything children leave behind: first, hide the item. To spring the item from junk jail, its owner has to do an extra chore. Even young children will get in the habit of removing their things from the car.
9. Toss a handful of canvas shopping bags into the car so that even if you leave the house without them you'll have some handy.

## How can I organize my wardrobe closet?

The first step is to decide which clothes you use, love, and want to store. Once you know that, organizing becomes much easier. Gather seven containers like laundry baskets or bags and clearly label them Toss, Repair, Give Away, Memory, Goes Somewhere Else, Store, and Keep.

Pull out articles of clothing one at a time and place them in one of the designated containers.

- Toss: Clothes you're not keeping and that aren't good enough to give away
- Repair: Clothes that need a button, tailoring, hemming, etc.
- Give Away: Clothes you no longer need, but are still good
- Memory: Clothes you want to keep but will not wear
- Goes Somewhere Else: Clothes that belong to someone else or that belong somewhere else in the house
- Store: Clothes you want to save for future use
- Keep: Clothes that you like and that fit

Have a pad of paper on hand as you sort the clothes. If you need to let go of something but you want a replacement, write it down.

And if you are missing any basics, write that down. You also can note what you plan to wear for special occasions or holidays.

Once you have pared down your wardrobe, choose how to store it. You don't need to hire a fancy custom closet company to redesign your space. Many home goods stores sell do-it-yourself closet organizing systems. Make sure to carefully measure your closet before buying a system so you can be sure it will fit.

One of the most effective closet organizing tools is a hanging rod that is at least 72 inches from the ground. It will allow you to hang a double hang rod for shirts and other items. If you install a shelf over the higher rod, use it to store rarely used pieces of clothing. A rod cover allows hangers to glide easily. Use sturdy hangers, with slip-proof material if needed.

Place clothing items in the closet, grouping them by type. Categories might include jeans and casual clothes, pants, dresses, and so on. Depending on what types of clothing you own, you might need a container that hangs from the closet rod and has compartments for sweaters, lingerie, or other items.

## My bathroom medicine cabinet is a big, jumbled mess. How can I make smaller items more accessible?

Glue a few small magnets to the inside of the cabinet. You can then attach tweezers and other small metal instruments like an eyelash curler.

## What are some suggestions for storing pet items?

Pets bring much joy—and clutter—into our lives. To minimize your pet clutter, first make a cleaning/care caddy. This is where you'll store all the items needed to clean and care for your pet. A dog owner would store nail clippers, a brush, and shampoo. An aquarium lover would have a water purifier, hoses, and extra filter inserts. Since these items are used occasionally, store the pet caddy on a shelf in the linen closet, in the garage, or in a kitchen cabinet. Everyday pet items need a home, too. Hang dog leashes on a hook near the door, and place fish food near the tank. Pet toys, like bones and balls, can be tucked away in an end table drawer or possibly in an ottoman if the lid lifts up for storage. Pet medications should never be stored near human medications. Instead, designate a small plastic bin or shoe box for pet medications and tuck it away somewhere like the top shelf in a hall closet. Finally, all pet-related paperwork, like proofs of vaccination, aquarium filter instruction manuals, and other necessary papers can be stored away in a three-ring binder filled with a few clear plastic sheet protectors. Simply slide the important papers into the protectors and keep the notebook on a centrally located bookshelf for reference.

## How can I disguise the cables for all the electronics we charge every day?

Concealing unsightly cords is a simple way to make a space look more organized instantly. There are two simple options depending on your decor and style. The first option is to use a decorative box. Try shopping at home first; you might already have a box you can repurpose. Cut a small hole in the back of the box and slip the plug end of a power strip through the hole. Plug the power strip into the wall outlet. Now you'll be able to plug in all the items you use. When the chargers aren't in use, put the lid on the box to conceal them. An alternative is to use Velcro tape to adhere a power strip to the back wall of a bookshelf. Then you can place all the electronics on the shelf and have a single location to plug them in. Ideally, this bookshelf is near your home's entryway so it's easily accessible. Allocate one shelf for electronics, one for outgoing items like mail, and maybe even a shelf for your purse, briefcase, or diaper bag.

## How can I organize my recycling?

Depending on where you live, there are different requirements for what and how to recycle. Major categories in recyclables are cans, cardboard, newspapers, glasses, and plastics. Set up a collection location in your home, usually in the kitchen, where you can keep a limited amount of recyclables before taking them out to the larger collection area outside your home or in the garage. Since kitchens are usually short on a space, creative solutions might be three small plastic containers under the sink or a slim floor-to-ceiling bookshelf with clearly labeled baskets on each shelf. If your budget and space permit, opt for a freestanding recycling unit purchased from a local home goods store. Recycling bins are cleverly disguised in the cabinet, and you can use the top of the cabinet for more kitchen storage.

*Chapter 5* **PAPER**

- What's the best way to store clippings from catalogs, magazines, and newspapers?
- How can I organize the piles of clippings and notes I use for scrap-booking?
- How can I best store/sort/discard my magazine collection?
- What's the best way to organize my catalogs?
- How can I stop printing stuff like emails and recipes?
- What's the best way to deal with junk mail?
- How can I keep my name and address off junk mail lists?
- How can I keep receipts organized in my purse without shoving them into my already overstuffed wallet?
- Is there a system for keeping track of my receipts at home?
- How can I organize my paid and unpaid bills?
- I need to leave important paper piles out as a visual reminder, but then the papers I need get lost in the pile. What can I do?
- How long should I keep important papers before I shred them?
- Which important papers belong in disaster-proof storage?
- How should I organize the papers I need in case of a medical emergency?
- How can I store manuals and warranties so I can easily reference them when I need them?
- How can I store bills that are due and remember to pay them on time?
- My finances are a mess. How can I organize all of those important papers?
- How can I balance my checkbook?
- Will paying bills online help me stay organized?
- What should I do with my medical paperwork?

## What's the best way to store clippings from catalogs, magazines, and newspapers?

First, determine what you're clipping and why. Clippings from catalogs are usually for future reference (a dining room table you think would be perfect for your home, or something that would be a great gift for Nana Sue). Place future reference clippings in a file folder with a proper label like Home Ideas or Gift Ideas.

Clipping magazine articles is another issue. Keep in mind that many magazine articles are cyclical—the same information this month is likely coming out the same month next year, but the information will be more current. So why save the article? If you need the article before next year, you can find it online or order a back issue of the magazine. Exceptions are useful articles you need soon, like an article on summer day trips. Put the magazine articles you're sure you want to save in a clearly labeled file folder.

When it comes to newspaper clippings, again, save only those you truly need. You can always access newspaper articles online. You can store newspaper clippings in one of two ways for quick retrieval: (1) a 4 x 6 inch index card box (use the tabs for topics, fold the clipping and tuck it in the correct section, or (2) a clippings binder (use a three-ring notebook filled with sheet protectors and slip the clipping in the clear plastic sheet protector). Another option for capturing all those great ideas as you read is to keep a single spiral notebook to jot everything down

## How can I organize the piles of clippings and notes I use for scrapbooking?

A good system for containing these pieces of paper is to create a craft notebook. Fill a three-ring binder with clear plastic sheet protectors, notepaper, a pocket folder, and a clear plastic pencil pouch. Slide articles, magazine clips, and your written ideas into the sheet protectors. Use the pouch for pens, markers, and little scraps, and place project pieces and ideas into the folder pockets. You might be able to contain all of your scrapbook items into a single notebook, but don't overstuff it. If necessary, make a few subcategory craft notebooks. Clearly label the outside spines and keep them within reach of your workstation.

## How can I best store/sort/discard my magazine collection?

Magazines tend to fall into one of two categories: read and recycle, or reference. Limit your subscriptions and checkout line purchases to only the magazines you love and make time to read. If you buy a magazine and don't read it, you're wasting your money. If you have subscriptions to similar types of magazines and you're not reading them, have the remaining issues sent to a friend, family member, salon, local assisted living community, or somewhere else where it has a better chance of being read. Keep the magazines you do read in a small basket or decorative container near where you read them. When a new issue arrives, recycle the old one—whether you've read it or not. Magazines are cyclical; this month's articles probably will be repeated next year at the same time, but with more current information. Reference magazines and professional journals can be stored in magazine files on a bookshelf. The key is to limit them to a specific quantity, like two years' worth of issues. Otherwise, the magazines will take up too much space. If you just can't part with magazines because you think you'll eventually read them, place them in a box, label it, tape it shut, and store it for six months. If you have time to read the magazines within six months, you can. If not, you can recycle them without guilt or donate them to a local library.

## What's the best way to organize my catalogs?

The best place to start is to eliminate your name from mailing lists of catalogs you don't wish to receive. This once belabored process has been simplified, thanks to www.catalogchoice.org. Instead of contacting each catalog company to have your name and address removed from the database, you can register for free with Catalog Choice and simply search the catalog database, checking the ones you no longer want to receive.

There's an easy way to deal with the catalog you want to keep. When the mail arrives, grab the catalogs and place them somewhere to read. You might pop them into a tote bag and grab the tote the next time you may have to wait for a doctor's appointment or to pick up a child from school. You can spend that time skimming your catalogs. Once you're done with the catalog, put it in one of three places:

1.  The recycling bin
2.  A basket or container with other catalogs you plan to order from. (When you add a new catalog, pull out the outdated one.)
3.  A magazine holder on your bookshelf where you keep reference catalogs with pages marked for ideas and inspiration

## How can I stop printing stuff like emails and recipes?

It's hard to resist printing the interesting things you find online. However, often these printed items end up in a pile, never to be seen again. Chances are, you've been surprised to come across something you printed months or even years earlier that you had forgotten about. Printing something doesn't mean you'll remember it or find it when you need it.

A solution is to save the information electronically instead. If you're not comfortable with computers, this might seem like a scary proposition, but once you try it you'll be hooked. It's simple. While on the web page you want to save, choose "file" then "save as." Then, like any other document you'd save, choose where to save it, and it will be automatically saved as a web page. To keep things organized, create one folder for all your saved pages, giving it a broad category name like House Ideas or Health Info, for example. When you save a page to the folder, it is imperative that you rename it so you'll know exactly what it is when you go back to look for it later. Another option is to copy the text from the web page and then paste it into a Word file. Then you can save the Word file like you would any other document.

Because websites change often, don't opt for bookmarking the web page instead of saving it. The page might be removed and not available when you return to the site.

## What's the best way to deal with junk mail?

The best way to deal with junk mail is to stop it from coming in the first place. What most people call junk mail is actually the result of direct marketing campaigns designed to get you to buy a product or service. It's called direct marketing because it attempts to match you and your buying preferences directly with offers that are likely to make you buy a product or service. When you purchase a product or service and give the company your name and address, chances are you'll be added to one or more mailing lists used for direct marketing. This is true when you buy a car or a house, use a shopping card, sign up for a credit card, subscribe to a magazine, buy something from a catalog, give money to a charity, or fill out a product registration form.

You can have your name and address removed from organizations' mailing lists by registering for the Mail Preference Service. When you register, your name and address are placed in a "do not mail" file that is updated monthly and distributed to direct marketers. If you are only going to do one thing to organize the paper you accumulate, this is the one to do. Send a signed letter plus a one-dollar check or money order to: Mail Preference Service, Direct Marketing Association, P.O. Box 282, Carmel, NY 10512. Include a short note expressing your wishes or fill in the form letter at http://jamienovak. com/Resources.html. If you prefer to register online, visit www. dmaconsumers.org/cgi/offmailinglist. You can also register the names of the deceased with the Deceased Do Not Contact list (DDNC) at https://www.dmachoice.org/consumerassistance.php.

No matter which opt-out method you choose, you can help make it more thorough by including every variation of your name and mailing address. For example, one piece of junk mail may be addressed to Jane Smith, another to Jane R. Smith, and yet another to Jayne Smith. Keep a running list of these variations and enclose it with your removal form or simply clip off the addressee part of the envelopes and staple them to your form. If you register online, just type in the variations.

It might take a month or so for the changes to take effect, but eventually you'll see a huge drop in the junk mail items you receive, sometimes up to 70 percent.

### Preapproved credit card offers

These preapproved offers contain your personal information, so be sure to shred them if you don't want to accept the offer. You can also have your name removed from the mailing lists. The federal Fair Credit Reporting Act (FCRA, 15 USC 1681) requires credit reporting companies to delete any consumer's name and address from mailing lists if the consumer so chooses. To opt out of the lists for five years or permanently, call (888) 5-OPT-OUT (888-567-8688) and use the automated system to enter your information. If you prefer to opt out online, go to www.optoutprescreen.com. Opting out of the preap-proval offers only means that you will not be solicited; it doesn't affect your ability to receive credit that you request.

## Sweepstakes and prizes

Contact the following sweepstakes companies directly to be removed from their mailing lists:

Publishers Clearinghouse
Christopher L. Irving, Sr. Director
Consumer & Privacy Affairs
Publishers Clearinghouse
382 Channel Drive
Port Washington, NY 11050
(800) 645-9242
privacychoices@pchmail.com

Readers Digest Sweepstakes
Reader's Digest
P.O. Box 50005
Prescott, AZ 86301-5005
(800) 310-6261

## Charities and nonprofits

Charities and nonprofit groups often rent or exchange each other's lists. When you fill out the form that goes with your donation, see if there's a box to check indicating that you don't want your name sold or rented. Checking that box will reduce similar solicitations. If you don't find an opt-out box to check, enclose a note requesting that the organization not rent, sell, or exchange your name and address. Before donating, you might wish to check the rating of the charity. The higher the rating, the smaller the amount of your donation goes to administrative costs and the larger amount to the actual cause. Charities with higher ratings don't make most of their money selling mailing lists. You can check a charity's rating at www. charitynavigator.org. Because many nonprofits rent lists from other groups, they do not keep the lists themselves and therefore cannot delete your name. Save the mailing label and the "reply device" from these mailings. They are likely to contain codes that indicate the list your name came from. Ask the organization that mailed you the solicitation for the name of the organization that rented the list. Then contact that organization and ask that your name not be rented, sold, or exchanged.

### *Junk mail addressed to "Resident" or "Occupant," like grocery store flyers*

**Valassis**
(888) 241-6760
P.O. Box 249
Windsor, CT 06095
www.advo.com/consumersupport.html

**PennySaver (CA)**
Circulation
c/o Pennysaver
2830 Orbiter Street
Brea, CA 92821
(800) 422-4116

**The Flyer (FL)**
Circulation
c/o Flyer
201 Kelsey Lane
Tampa, FL 33619
(813) 626-SELL

**Val-Pak Savings Coupons**

For blue envelope only: www.coxtarget.com/mailsuppression/s/
DisplayMailSuppressionForm

For any other color envelope, contact the address on the envelope as they are regional and not national.

### Mail order catalogs, free magazines

Abacus database (you'll need your name, including any middle initial; your current address; and if you've moved recently, your previous address)

Abacus, Inc.
P.O. Box 1478
Broomfield, CO 80038
By email: abacusoptout@epsilon.com

## How can I keep my name and address off junk mail lists?

Be aware of the three sneaky ways companies gather your information, probably without your even knowing it:

1. Often, when the cashier at a store asks for your phone number, it means the company will use that number to look up your mailing address and add it to its database. Decline to give your phone number.
2. The U.S. Postal Service provides the addresses from its change of address cards to major marketing and financial companies. The Postal Service's goal is to have less misaddressed mail, which translates to informing junk mailers where you live. You might consider not filling out the change of address card when you move. This will mean a little more work for you, since you'll have to contact all of your important correspondents individually. In the long run, however, that

legwork might be worth it since you won't be forced to deal with unwanted mail for years to come.

3. Product registration cards and consumer surveys seem innocent enough; you buy a new digital camera and fill out and mail the postage-paid registration card as directed. However, warranty or product registration cards have less to do with warranties than they do with mailing lists. These cards often ask about your hobbies, the number of people in your household, your income, and other information the company obviously does not need to guarantee the product. A dead giveaway is to notice the card's address—most registration cards are mailed to a post office box in Denver, Colorado, and not to the company that manufactured the product. The Colorado company compiles buyer profiles and sells the information to other companies for marketing purposes. Read the fine print on the registration card; it usually has a statement informing you that failure to complete and return the card does not diminish your warranty rights, and that your dated receipt serves as your proof of purchase.

## How can I keep receipts organized in my purse without shoving them into my already overstuffed wallet?

A simple envelope is a great temporary storage solution for receipts. You can use a regular mailing envelope to get started, but it will not stand up well to wear and tear over time. A sturdier long-term solution is a small plastic envelope with a Velcro closure, available at office supply stores.

## Is there a system for keeping track of my receipts at home?

Unless your tax professional gives you other instructions, you should save receipts until you check them against your checking account or credit card statement.. To set up a receipt station, label a few letter-size envelopes with the types of payment you commonly use. For example, you might label the envelopes VISA, American Express, Debit, and VISA Gold.

Label the back of the envelope instead of the front to save yourself a step—since you fill the envelope from the back, you won't have to flip it over to read the label. If you prefer color-coding, use a different color of envelope for each category.

Next, place the envelopes in a box or basket near where you stop as you come in the house, such as the kitchen or entryway. Each time you make a purchase, place the receipt in a single envelope in your purse or wallet. As you enter your house, stop at the receipt station, pull the receipts from you purse or wallet, and place them in the correct envelope. When it's time to pay bills, match the receipts from the envelopes to the correct statements. Clip the receipts to the appropriate statements and file them away. A multiple-pocket accordion folder labeled by month works well. At the end of the year, write the year on the front of the accordion folder and file it away with your tax return.

This system will make it easy to find receipts for large purchases if you ever need to reference them. You might be surprised to find some mistakes as you check your statements. Many people report finding "lost" money. Examples include double billing at a gas station, overtipping at a restaurant, unauthorized debits, and automatic debits you thought had been stopped but are still being billed.

## How can I organize my paid and unpaid bills?

Try auto debit and online banking if you haven't already—they are the best ways to streamline the bill-paying process. If you get paper bills, designate one place to collect them all. Open the bill, toss the inserts, and keep only the bill and return envelope.

Place the bills in a single location, a bill-paying basket, a box with envelopes for receipts, a single file in a desktop file box, or some other location. You can make it even easier by having a pen, calculator, stamps, and checkbook in the same location. Pay the bill, then keep the stub for one month so you can check that you were properly credited when next month's bill arrives. After that, either shred the stub or place it in an accordion file, in the pocket for that month. Do what you are most comfortable with or your tax professional suggests.

## I need to leave important paper piles out as a visual reminder, but then the papers I need get lost in the pile. What can I do?

Here's what you're going to need to whip your paper piles into shape:

- Desktop file box with no lid (you can see a full line of boxes a www.JamieNovak.com; they are also available at most office supply stores)
- Set of hanging folders (any color)
- Pad of 2 x 2 inch sticky notes
- Pen
- Calendar

Even if you don't have all the items listed above, you can start setting up your file box system. Follow these steps:

1. To get started, set your kitchen timer for eighteen minutes. You probably won't finish in that time, but you'll make a serious dent in the paper pile.
2. Grab a handful of the most recent pending paperwork from the countertops and tables. You won't be able to go through

all the piles today. Your goal is to work for at least eighteen minutes, not to finish.

3. Sit down and separate the papers into file folders by category, like bills, items to read, photos, coupons, receipts, and so on. Do not make mini piles. Instead, place the papers directly into a file folder so that if you get interrupted and have to step away, the piles you've made won't get mixed up again.

4. As you sort your papers into file folders, throw away obviously unnecessary stuff like expired coupons. Don't spend too much time making decisions about the papers, however. This is not the time to think about whether to keep it or toss it. It's also not the time to think about whether you want to go to the party you've been invited to. Instead, toss the invitation into a file with similar papers. Note: You'll probably make some duplicate files at this stage. Don't worry; you can always consolidate later.

5. Use a sticky note to label each file folder by attaching the sticky part of the note to the file and leaving the rest sticking up as the label. Don't dwell over folder names, just write something that will help you remember what's inside. Avoid labeling folders Important, Pending, This Week, and Urgent, since so many of the papers potentially fall into those categories. Instead use names like Sports Schedules, Invitations, Scouts, and so on. A more complete list is below.

6. The final step is to note on the calendar anything that needs your attention. That way, you won't have to sift through each file every day to see what needs your attention. For example, if you need to register your child for swim lessons by the twentieth of the month, make a note on the calendar about a week earlier, "swim registration—paper in swim folder."

Here is an example of how a paper might flow through your new system:

In today's mail you receive a community school brochure that you'd like to browse. You may or may not register for a class; you need to read the brochure first. Open the brochure to the registration page to find the registration deadline. Write a note on your calendar about a week before the deadline to remind yourself to read the brochure and that it will be in the community school folder.

Write "community school" on a sticky note. Put the note on a file folder, put the brochure inside, and tuck it away in your file box. When the date rolls around, you'll see the note on the calendar reminding you that you need to read the brochure. At that point, take the brochure with you so you can glance at it in your spare time. If nothing catches your eye, then toss the brochure. If you see something you want to register for, then do so. Write the date of the class on the calendar.

Next, place the brochure back in the community school file, since you'll probably need to refer to it on the day of the class for pertinent information.

These file folders live in the box for a short time—the summer camp folder stays only until you register for summer camp or camp is over. Other folders, like those for bills and receipts, remain in the box but their contents stay for only a short time. That's why you use sticky notes for labels instead of the plastic tabs. Other folders capture items that will be moved to long-term files, like investment statements. By placing them in this folder temporarily, you can keep track of them before moving them to the permanent file.

Here are some examples of the folders you can create:

• A file for each family member
• Babysitter: Things your babysitter needs to know

- Bake sale
- Banking: Deposit and withdrawal receipts for that month, monthly statement to be reconciled
- Birthday party
- Books to read: Lists of books you'd like to read and book reviews
- Clippings: Newspaper or magazine clippings that don't fit another category but would be good to refer to at some point
- Contacts: Business cards and scraps of paper with names and numbers
- Coupons: Coupons and gift certificates
- Cub Scouts
- Day trips: Brochures and ideas for day trips
- Directions: Either handwritten or printed from a website
- Discussion: Things to ask your spouse about
- Entertainment: Tickets to events and newspaper clippings of upcoming events
- Family meeting: Topics to be discussed
- Gifts: Ideas for gifts for others or your own wish list; pictures clipped from catalogs stapled to the order information
- Grocery shopping: Sales flyers, shopping list, food store coupons
- Hairstyle ideas
- Halloween costumes
- Health: Kids' medical records, prescriptions, physician referrals
- Holiday card writing
- Household: Warranties and instruction manuals
- Instructions: Clippings of a craft pattern, cake-decorating tips, or other directions
- Investments: Brokerage house statements
- Kitchen remodel
- Landscaping
- Memory box: Artwork and other items to be saved in a treasure box

- Movies: A list of movies you'd like to see and reviews of them
- Online: Websites that you would like to check out someday
- Pay stubs: Pay stubs or direct deposit statements
- Photos: Photos to be put into an album
- PTA
- Receipts
- Restaurants: Restaurants you want to try and reviews
- Schedules: Sports schedules, recycling calendars, event calendars
- School: Lunch tickets, schoolwork in progress, school calendar
- Social engagements: Party invitations, directions to events
- Spiritual: Schedules of events
- Take-out menus: Menus and coupons for local restaurants
- Taxes: Items needed for upcoming tax filing
- To file: Select papers that will be moved to a permanent file
- To read: Magazine articles, newsletters
- Travel: Brochures, ideas for places to visit

You might need some or all of these categories; your box should be personalized according to your needs. Remember that this system will be successful only if you put papers in and take papers out. Otherwise you'll outgrow your box within a week. Try reviewing the box on Saturday mornings or while watching TV. Remove outdated papers to keep the folders up to date.

## How long should I keep important papers before I shred them?

Here is a general list that includes the type of paper, when you should toss it, and where to keep it in the meantime. This is just a general list; always check with your tax professional before discarding important papers.

## Banking

- ATM receipts: Keep until recorded in checkbook; store in box in entryway or in dresser-top basket as received
- Bank-deposit slips: Keep until after you reconcile your statements; store in box in entryway or dresser top basket as received
- Bank statements: Keep for one year; store in accordion file folder with slots labeled for each month
- Bills (paid): Keep for one year; store in accordion file folder with slots labeled for each month
- Canceled checks: Keep for one year; seven years for checks supporting taxes; store in accordion file folder with slots labeled for each month
- Certificates of deposit: Keep until maturity; store in safe-deposit box or home disaster-proof box
- Check registers: Keep for one year; store in accordion file folder with slots labeled for each month
- Credit card statements: Keep for one year; seven years if supporting taxes; store in accordion file folder with slots labeled for each month
- Loan documents: Keep until loan is repaid; store in home filing cabinet
- Loan-discharge notices: Never discard; store in safe-deposit box or home disaster-proof box
- Pay stubs: Save only the newest one and shred the older ones

## Estate

- Health-care proxy: Save newest version only; store in safe-deposit box or home disaster-proof box; include contact information for primary-care physician, attorney, and anyone named to make decisions on your behalf

- Living trust: Save newest version only; store in safe-deposit box or home disaster-proof box with contact information for successor trustee, attorney
- Living will: Save newest version only: store in safe-deposit box or home disaster-proof box with contact information for attorney, executor
- Power of attorney: Save newest version only; store in safe-deposit box or home disaster-proof box with contact information for designee, attorney
- Will: Save newest version only: store in safe-deposit box or home disaster-proof box with contact information for attorney, executor

## Insurance

- Annually renewed insurance policies: Keep newest version only; store in home filing cabinet
- Explanation of benefits: Keep as long as you have the policy; store in home filing cabinet
- Insurance inventory: Keep newest version only; store in safe-deposit box or home disaster-proof box
- Permanent life (whole life, etc.): Keep forever; store in safe-deposit box or home disaster-proof box
- Term life: Discard after the term expires; store in safe-deposit box or home disaster-proof box

## Investments

- Brokerage statements: Keep until you sell the securities, then hold with your tax return for seven years: household filing cabinet
- Deed: Keep as long as you own the property; store in safe-deposit box or home disaster-proof box
- Purchase confirmations and 1099s: Keep until securities are sold, then put with your tax returns; household filing cabinet

- Savings bonds: Keep until maturity; store in safe-deposit box or home disaster-proof box and keep a list of numbers at home

## *Personal*
- Birth certificate: Keep forever; store in safe-deposit box or home disaster-proof box
- Death certificates: Keep forever; store in safe-deposit box or home disaster-proof box
- Marriage license: Keep forever; store in safe-deposit box or home disaster-proof box
- Military discharge papers: Keep forever: store in safe-deposit box or home disaster-proof box
- Social Security card: Keep forever; store in safe-deposit box or home disaster-proof box

## *Product purchases*
- Car title: Keep until you sell the vehicle; store in safe-deposit box or home disaster-proof box
- Receipts: Keep until warranty expires; keep for seven years if needed to support tax returns; staple to warranty booklet
- Warranties: Keep until warranty expires; store in slotted accordion file folder

## *Retirement*
- 401(k) statements: Keep newest statement only; store in household filing cabinet
- Employer defined-benefit plan communications: Keep forever; store in household filing cabinet
- Social Security statements: Keep newest one only: store in household filing cabinet

### *Taxes*
- Personal state and federal tax returns and supporting documents: Keep for seven years; store in household filing cabinet

## Which important papers belong in disaster-proof storage?

Here is a suggested list of papers that need to be protected from damage. They can be stored in a disaster-proof storage box in your home or in a safe-deposit box at a bank. If you plan to use a safe-deposit box at a bank, consider the hours of the bank to ensure it will be open if you need the items. As a double security measure, you also might want to store a duplicate copy of important papers at a friend's or family member's house.

- Automobile insurance cards and policies
- Bank account numbers
- Car registrations and titles
- Cemetery plot deeds
- Certificates of birth or death
- Copy of driver's license
- Credit card account numbers and companies
- Homeowner's policy
- Household inventory
- Immunization records
- Important telephone numbers
- Insurance cards and policies
- Investment records
- Legal papers (such as divorce decrees and property settlement papers)
- Life insurance policy
- Mailing list of family and friends

- Marriage licenses
- Medical history
- Military records
- Papers or records that prove ownership (such as real estate deeds, automobile titles, and stock and bond certificates)
- Passports
- Personal identification numbers (PINs)
- Photo negatives, one wedding photo, and one baby photo
- Residency letter (a letter from the state sent to you at current address to prove you reside there)
- Social Security cards
- Tax records
- Will/living will or advance directive, or Durable Powers of Attorney for Health Care

## How should I organize the papers I need in case of a medical emergency?

Create a medical emergency grab-and-go file. It will provide peace of mind in the event that someone in your home is in need of emergency medical treatment. Place the following information in a brightly colored file folder and store it on a bookshelf. Make sure each family member knows where it is.

- Allergies (including food, medications, and latex)
- Current medical conditions
- Current medications (including vitamins and supplements)
- Immunizations (including tetanus)
- Insurance information
- Mini medical history (including surgeries)
- Physicians' names and numbers
- Signed medical consent form (In the event you are not the one

bringing your child(ren) to the hospital, this signed letter allows for treatment.)

You can find printable consent forms at The American College of Emergency Physicians, www.ACEP.org. Choose the Patients Center tab, Emergency Manual, and then Medical Forms.

## How can I store manuals and warranties so I can easily reference them when I need them?

There are three possible solutions. Choose the one you think will work best for you.

1.  Store them in an accordion file. Label the sections with categories, then tie up the file and store it on a bookshelf or closet shelf.
2.  Store them in a three-ring binder with clear plastic sheet protectors. Using one category per sheet protector, you can fit many manuals in the binder. You might want to make separate binders for different categories and then store them in the appropriate place, like the kitchen, the garage, or the playroom.
3.  Use one ziplock bag per item to hold the booklet, receipt, and any spare parts. Write the date on the front of the bag so you know what is most recent. Then store the bags in a decorative box, file drawer, or storage box under the bed. To simplify things, have two boxes, one marked A-M and the other N-Z, and sort the bags by the name of the item.

Maintain your new system by going through the warranties and manuals files every time you change your clocks for daylight saving time. You don't need to keep a paper manual if the manual is available online. You can almost always go to the manufacturer's website to view and print the manual. If you have an extended warranty, however, you do need to keep the paperwork. When you buy a new product, simply slip the new manual into a sheet protector in your binder or into a slot in the accordion file.

## How can I store bills that are due and remember to pay them on time?

A bill caddy is a great spot to store incoming bills. Use a basket, tub, or other container and place it on the desk in your home office or on a shelf in the kitchen. If you're going to leave it in plain sight, make sure it has a lid so visitors can't see your personal information. Stock the caddy with stamps, return address labels, a pen, a calculator, and blank envelopes. Toss all bills into the caddy as you receive them. When you want to pay bills, just carry the caddy with you to any room of the house. Having a bill caddy will help you avoid making late payments or searching for bills that may or may not have arrived. Even if you pay your bills online, you can utilize this new system.

## My finances are a mess. How can I organize all of those important papers?

Here is a wonderful system that you can set up quickly and easily.

Gather the following items:

- Ten to fifteen hanging file folders
- Twenty-five to thirty file folders
- A marker

Step 1—Label each of the hanging folders with these titles:

- Tax Returns
- Retirement

- Social Security
- Investments
- Bank Accounts
- Household Accounts
- Credit Cards/Loans
- Insurance
- Wills/Trusts
- Children's Accounts

Step 2—Label the file folders to go inside each of the hanging folders:

### Tax returns
Label one folder for each of the past seven years, including one for the current year and one for next year. Then fill each folder with the tax returns. The file for the next year leaves you room to grow.

### Retirement
Label folders with the name of each financial institution that has your investment (401k, IRAs, etc.). Keep the quarterly and year-end statements.

### Social Security
Label one file folder for each person with a statement that comes from the government.

### Investments
Label one file per investment account. Examples include mutual funds, CDs, stocks, and brokerage accounts.

### Bank accounts
Label one file per checking and/or savings account.

### Household accounts

Label one file for your home title (or lease if you rent), home improvements, and mortgage.

### Credit cards/loans

Label one file per credit card, loan, student loan, and any other borrower.

### Insurance

Label one file per policy: health, life, car, homeowners, renter's, long-term care, etc.

### Wills/trusts

Label one file per will, trust, or living will along with instructions on where to find other important documents and lawyers' contact information.

### Children's accounts

Label one file folder per minor who has an account.

## How can I balance my checkbook?

Balancing a checkbook is easier than ever before. Since many people opt to pay with debit or credit cards rather than paper checks, they have fewer checks to track. If you have online banking, take a moment to check what options are available to you. You can even call the online customer service number and ask someone to walk you through some of the options. Most banks offer some form of free money management and reports for their customers.

At the end of the day, week, or month, you need to know that the money you put into your account and the money you took out match up with the receipts you have. As you balance your accounts, you might find discrepancies, some of which can be costly Double billing on a charge because the card was improperly swiped, an incorrect amount entered by the person processing the card, an incorrect deposit at the bank, or an automatic withdrawal you had forgotten about are just some examples. It makes sense to take some time every so often to balance the books. To do this, simply scan the credit card or bank account statement and look at the debits and credits. If anything looks suspicious, research it. If possible, have current receipts handy and tick them off as you locate them on the statement. You might be surprised at what you find. The biggest error for a client I've ever seen was for $30,000 when a bank deposit was incorrectly credited to another person's account. Needless to say, she was very happy she had her deposit slip to refer to, and the few moments it took her to scan the statement really paid off.

## Will paying bills online help me stay organized?

Yes, online bill paying can save you time and lots of money. Not only will you save on stamps, but you can schedule payments in advance so there's no chance of forgetting them. Imagine having all your bills in the queue to be paid without having to do a thing. With online bill pay, there are no more piles of bills to be paid, no more searching for the checkbook and calculator, and no more licking envelopes and stamps. Additionally, many banks now offer money management reports at a glance, which means you can enter your information once and then view graphs showing where your money is going. Organizing your finances has never been easier.

## What should I do with my medical paperwork?

Medical paperwork is perhaps the most unpleasant paperwork to deal with. That's because having medical paperwork usually means there is an issue with your health or the health of a loved one. Plus, medical paperwork can be extremely confusing.

Make the process of dealing with medical papers as simple as possible by grabbing a single file folder. On the tab write a meaningful title so you'll know what's inside. Instead of a generic phrase like Medical Paperwork, try something more specific like Benefit Statements. As you get new correspondence, such as an explanation of benefits from the insurance company or a new statement from the physician, place it in the front of the file. That way, the most recent correspondence is always on top when you open the folder. As papers come in, you can staple or clip together the ones that go together, like a physician's statement and an explanation of what was paid by the insurance company. Another great tip is to write the physician and insurance company contact information on the front of the folder. The next time you need to make a call about something, all of the information will be handy. If you get thrown into an automated phone system, jot down the sequence of numbers you need to push to get to a live person. That will make your next call much shorter.

*Chapter 6*    # STORAGE

- What are some suggestions for safe photo storage?
- How should I store digital photos?
- What's the best way to store out-of-season clothing?
- I live in an older home that lacks closet space. What can I do for storage?
- I don't have an attic or basement. Without renting space, how can I store things?
- I want to store my adult child's toys for my grandchildren to use one day. What's the safest solution?
- How can I store oversized seasonal items, such as sporting equipment?
- What can I do with all the greeting cards I've accumulated?
- What's the best way to store greeting cards I plan to send someday?
- What should I do with the replacement buttons and thread clipped from my new clothing tags?
- Is there a convenient way to store shoes without buying an entire closet organizer system?

## What are some suggestions for safe photo storage?

Here are basic steps for keeping photographs safe:

1.  Collect all your photos and put them in a safe spot.
2.  Collect all your negatives and put them in a safe spot, away from your photos in case something happens to the photos.
3.  Make a plan to sort them.
4.  Store negatives in acid-free envelopes or polypropylene pockets.
5.  Store photos in acid-free boxes or in polypropylene pockets, or adhere them to acid-free pages.
6.  Turn the chore into a fun social gathering by inviting friends or family to sort their own photos with you.

To avoid damaging photos, keep the following in mind:

1.  Don't store photos in your basement or attic. Extremes in temperature can damage them.
2.  Don't store photos where the humidity is over 70 percent (they can mildew) or under 40 percent (they can become brittle).
3.  Don't expose photos to direct sunlight.
4.  Don't place photos into magnetic pages in photo albums; the glue will ruin the photos.
5.  Don't adhere photos to black photo pages. The pages are not acid-free and can damage the photos.
6.  Don't write on the back of photos with a ballpoint pen. It breaks the emulsion and can bleed through. Instead, use a photo-safe pen.
7.  Don't leave photos in a jumbled mess. Instead work in small yet consistent blocks of time to tackle piles of photos.

# How should I store digital photos?

Many people have attempted to simplify photo storage by going digital, only to find that having digital photos doesn't eliminate overwhelming organizational issues. To store and retrieve digital photos, you must develop a system. Make it a habit to download your photos the same day you take them, no matter what. (If you are not sure how to download them, have someone help you or read your digital camera manual. Camera manufacturers usually have a toll-free number you can call for assistance.) As soon as you download photos from your camera, delete the ones that aren't so great. Or, even better, delete the not-so-great shots as you take the photos.

### Storing photos on your computer

You can create file folders on your computer with event names and dates and store the photos in them. Or, opt for photo organizing software. For example, say you just took Thanksgiving photos, along with a few photos of fall foliage and a shot or two while holiday shopping. Store like with like by naming a folder November 2009. Think of this folder as a hanging folder. Inside the hanging folder create subfolders, like manila folders, named Thanksgiving 2009, Fall Foliage 2009, and Holiday Shopping 2009.

Name each photo inside the folders. Give them captions such as "dinner table set for holiday menu," "oak tree in front yard," "Aunt Sue shopping in Macy's," and so on.

The key is consistency. Whatever the new file naming system is, follow it regularly. If you fall a little behind, catch up instead of continuing to fall even further behind.

### Printing photos

You can save digital photos to be printed to a CD or a removable storage device like a flash drive, then simply take them to a local drugstore or home goods store that offers on-site digital printing. Alternately, you easily can upload the photos from your computer to a website like www.snapfish.com, www.Kodak.com, www. shutterfly.com, or www.fujifilm.com, and choose home delivery or pick up from a local participating drugstore. This method works especially well if you want to send photos to friends and family who live far away; you can have them printed at a drugstore near the recipient. You also can print digital photos yourself on your home printer using photo paper.

### Archiving photos

To store the photos somewhere other than on your computer, you can burn them onto a CD. Then once you have labeled it, store the CD in a CD case. Again store like photos together, and make a CD of the same types of photo. Try not to burn photos of a wedding and of a holiday onto the same CD.

Make duplicate copies of CDs containing special photos, and store them at someone else's home or in a disaster-proof storage box. Also, make sure to back up your computer. If you don't back up the files, your photos might be lost in the event of a major crash.

## What's the best way to store out-of-season clothing?

First and foremost, whenever possible stay away from large plastic tubs for storing clothing. They are usually too bulky to move and difficult to maneuver into storage areas, and you might not be lucky enough to have enough space for them. Instead opt for smaller storage containers, which are much easier to carry and store, and allow you to store like with like (a basic organizing principle). You can keep jeans in one, and turtlenecks in another. When the seasons start to change, you can bring out just what you need instead of lugging out a huge bin and living out of it for a few weeks.

## I live in an older home that lacks closet space. What can I do for storage?

When a home has limited closet space, you simply need to be a little more creative. Armoires can double as a closet. Bookshelves and other chests can store things as well. Decorative baskets with lids can house other items. Hanging items is another way to capitalize on otherwise wasted space. Use your vertical space. For example, go with a floor-to-ceiling bookcase instead of a shorter one that has fewer shelves and whose top collects clutter. Another option is to use hooks or nails on walls to hang things. Here are other ways to make up for a lack of closet space:

- Buy multipurpose furniture; for example, an ottoman that opens for storage or a trunk or chest that doubles as a coffee table.
- Store items on the backs of room doors and the insides of cabinet doors.
- Use the perimeter of the room. Install shelves eighteen inches below the ceiling on all or some of the walls.
- Store items under the bed.
- Hang items like pots and pans.
- Place a floor-length tablecloth over a decorator table to create a hidden storage area underneath.
- Create a makeshift mudroom by placing an armoire in or near the home's entryway. The armoire doors can still hold hooks, and the shelving and hanging space will come in handy. If adding an armoire would make the walkway too narrow, see if it is possible to recess the armoire into a wall.
- Another way to create a mudroom is to place a baker's rack near the entryway. Store items in the shelves and cabinets.
- Use an armoire for storage in other small spaces. It can serve as a craft area, a home office, a work and tool area, a bar, a gardening area, a laundry station, and more.

- Make furniture substitutions to add storage options. Substitute a trunk for your living room coffee table. A trunk offers a large amount of storage and makes a distinct statement. An ottoman with storage space inside and a tray on top can double as a table or as extra seating. A small chest of drawers works well as an end table.
- Instead of buying new furniture, modify an existing coffee table or end table to make it more functional. Place a basket, container, or rolling bin beneath the table to make use of the previously wasted space.
- Store spare towels in the bathroom. If the bathroom is short on space, try one of these creative storage options. Roll the towels so you can fit more on the shelf. Store rolled towels in a wall-mounted towel rack or a wine rack. You can also purchase a towel stand, which fits about ten folded towels, or stand rolled towels on end in a basket.

## I don't have an attic or basement. Without renting space, how can I store things?

First of all, you'll need to cut back on the number of items you need to store, which is a good thing.

With limited space, you have to be storage savvy and carefully choose what to store. If you don't love an item enough to use it now, there's probably no reason to store it. Store the items that you do want to keep in full boxes only, and try to use boxes that stack well. Oddly shaped boxes can be difficult to stack without the risk of tipping.

Walk around your home and check higher storage spots. Look in your closets and see if you can add high shelves. Consider adding a shelf around the perimeter of a room about eighteen inches down from the ceiling, and store items there. Then look down. Look under dressers, under media cabinets, and under the bed for unused storage space.

Disguising storage space also is an option. Nobody will see boxes sitting under a side table if you have a floor-length tablecloth covering them. And don't forget the outside of your home; do you have space for a shed? Even a small one can provide tons of storage space.

## I want to store my adult child's toys for my grandchildren to use one day. What's the safest solution?

To keep a treasured toy collection safe for future generations, don't store the toys in the attic or in an airtight plastic bin. Fluctuating temperatures and moisture trapped in the plastic bin can spell disaster. (If you absolutely must use plastic bins, cut in a few air holes.) To store old toys properly, first make sure that they are free of dust and dirt. Then, wrap each one individually in white tissue paper and place the wrapped toys in sturdy cardboard boxes. Add silica packets to the boxes to absorb moisture. Silica packets are typically available at housewares stores, or you can recycle the packets that come with a new pair of shoes. They are harmful if swallowed, so use caution.

Put the boxes in a closet or under your bed to keep the contents in a controlled climate and out of direct sunlight. Place a cedar block or cedar clothes hanger (found at most grocery stores in the laundry aisle) above the boxes to keep pests away.

## How can I store oversized seasonal items, such as sporting equipment?

Storing things like camping equipment, scuba gear, skis, and golf clubs can be a challenge. If you have a garage or a basement, your best bet is to hang what you can on the walls or ceiling. You can buy budget-friendly specialty hooks designed just for this purpose. Or, invest in storage solutions like HyLoft or other overhead storage options sold at local home improvement stores. The walls of the garage or basement usually go virtually unutilized, but they can provide a tremendous amount of good storage space. If your home doesn't have a garage or basement, simply create your own out-of-the-way storage space. Buy a freestanding closet system from a local home improvement store or home goods store; they are well worth the money. Another option for instant storage space for large items is a small shed, which you can place in your yard or on the side of your home. Treat a shed as you would a garage, and use all the vertical wall space you can.

## What can I do with all the greeting cards I've accumulated?

Greeting cards are an unusual kind of clutter because many of them contain sentimental messages written by friends and loved ones, and they are usually given to you to mark a special occasion. In a way, the card becomes part of that special time. However, if you keep every single greeting card you receive, the truly special cards can get lost amid the mess. Try setting aside a few blocks of time over the next month to reminisce while flipping through the cards. As you read the cards, sort them into four bins, labeled Keep, Recycle, Family Member, or Crafts. The ones you'll keep will include those for once-in-a-lifetime events, like a new baby, first anniversary, graduation, and so on. Keepers also might include cards with a heartfelt handwritten note, rather than just a signature. Choose one decorative box as the place to keep the cards, and make sure to leave room for additional cards you receive. If a card is from someone you don't have a special attachment to, put it in the Recycle bin.

If your collection includes cards addressed to family members such as children, place the cards in a treasure box so they can look back on them in the future. If you enjoy crafts like scrapbooking, keep a small number of cards in the Craft bin or in a scrapbook album to use for those projects.

## What's the best way to store greeting cards I plan to send someday?

Use a multiple-slot accordion file folder to store the cards, a few postage stamps, and a handful of return address labels. That way, everything you need will be handy when you want to send a card. To stock the folder with cards, buy an assorted pack of greeting cards. Over the next year, whenever you purchase a card, buy one or two extra name-brand cards to keep in the folder. Then you'll have on hand both generic cards from the assorted pack and name-brand cards, creating a nice variety. You don't always have to use the cards from your stock, but they can sure come in handy when you're short on time. Here are the most common greeting card categories:

- Anniversary
- Baptism or Christening
- Bat/Bar Mitzvah
- Birthday
- Chanukah
- Christmas
- Congratulations
- Easter
- Encouragement
- Engagement
- Expecting
- Father's Day

- Friendship
- Get Well
- Good Luck
- Graduation
- Holiday
- Housewarming
- Loss of a Pet
- Miss You
- Mother's Day
- New Baby
- New Job
- New Year
- Passover
- Retirement
- Romance
- Rosh Hashanah
- St. Patrick's Day
- Sympathy
- Thanksgiving
- Thinking of You
- Valentine's Day
- Wedding

If you decide to store cards for all of these categories, make sure the accordion file you choose has enough pockets to house every category.

## What should I do with the replacement buttons and thread clipped from my new clothing tags?

First, decide if the buttons and thread are worth keeping. If you've never used replacements in the past, then you might want to discard them. If you want to keep them just in case, or because you use them for another purpose, then place them in an envelope or small box along with a small pair of scissors and a pen, and store the envelope or box in a dresser drawer. Whenever you clip a replacement button from a new piece of clothing, write the date and the article of clothing on the little plastic bag the button came in before tucking it in the envelope. Now it will be easy to find the buttons you need because they'll be marked, and you can easily discard older ones by date.

## Is there a convenient way to store shoes without buying an entire closet organizer system?

Shoes are best stored in your closet vertically, where you can easily get to them. If you have a hanging bar, purchase a canvas shelving unit that hangs from the bar. The only downside is that unless you tie the unit to the floor, it might swing, making it cumbersome to take shoes out and put them away. Another option is a slim floor-to-ceiling bookshelf. You can use the shelves to store pairs of shoes or shoe boxes with the shoes inside. Remember to measure your closet first to make sure a bookshelf will fit inside the closet doorframe as well as inside the closet. If you already have a shelf in the closet, you can add a twelve-, eighteen-, or twenty-four-slot shoe cubby made of a thick-coated cardboard or thin wood.

No matter which shoe storage method you choose, you won't be able to find your shoes if there isn't sufficient light in the closet. If you don't have a light in your closet, you don't need to hire an electrician to install one. Buy one of the bright, battery-operated lights on the market that attach with extra-sticky tape or a single nail. They are designed to stay cool enough to use in a closet.

# Chapter 7  KITCHEN

- How can I make meal planning easier?
- Is there a way to organize all the take-out menus that are jammed in my kitchen drawer?
- What is a master grocery list, and how does it work?
- How can I save time cooking?
- My coupon drawer is not working. I spend time clipping coupons but never use them. What can I do?
- My recipes are everywhere, and I never get around to using them. What are some suggestions?
- Our leftovers always go bad in the refrigerator because we forget to eat them. How can we avoid this?
- What's the best way to identify stuff in the freezer?
- How long can I freeze food?
- Is there any way to make kitchen cleanup faster?
- I can't find things in my refrigerator. What am I doing wrong?
- What's the best way to clean the refrigerator?
- How can I keep my spices organized in the cabinet?
- Where can I store place mats so they don't jam my drawers or get damaged?
- I can never find a pot holder when I need one. Any ideas?
- What are some tips for putting away clean dishes faster?
- I need more kitchen cabinet space. What are some suggestions?
- Can gadgets make my kitchen more disorganized?
- How can I cut down on the time I spend cooking?

## How can I make meal planning easier?

First, gather meal ideas. Survey family members, read take-out menus, flip through cookbooks, scan the recipes you've clipped or printed but never tried, and search online. Make a list of ten to twelve meal ideas. At this point don't worry about whether or not you can make the meal easily or if you even have the ingredients, just write down the ideas. Note: Family members will be more likely to eat the meals they suggest, so take their comments seriously.

Next, check your list of ideas to see which dishes use similar ingredients. That way, you can prepare the ingredient once and use it for multiple meals. For example, ground meat is needed to make both tacos and spaghetti with meat sauce. You can prepare the ground meat, then make tacos one day and spaghetti the next. If you make a double batch of penne pasta, you can use half for a pasta salad and the other half for penne with vodka sauce. Get creative with ways to make meals easier. Maybe instead of cooking lasagna noodles, you can opt for the no-boil version.

Check the recipes you've chosen and make a two-week shopping list by looking at the required ingredients for each of the meals you plan to cook. If your budget allows, give yourself a break on some days and plan to eat out or order take-out instead. Check your fridge, freezer, and pantry to see what ingredients you already have so you can cross them off your shopping list. Then go shopping, or log on to an online shopping site and have some or all of the items delivered.

This is important: Save your grocery list. It's a two-week meal plan and shopping list. Once you've made a few lists, then simply rotate them to save even more time.

## Is there a way to organize all the take-out menus that are jammed in my kitchen drawer?

Instead of a drawer, try housing them in a file folder tucked at the end of a counter. Weed out the duplicate menus and staple any coupons directly to the corresponding menus so you won't forget to use them. Also try keeping a duplicate set of menus in your car (also organized in a file folder) for those times when you want to place an order but you need to look at the menu or forgot the phone number.

## What is a master grocery list, and how does it work?

A master grocery list is a list of all the common items you usually purchase at the grocery store. Once the list is made, photocopy it and keep a copy hanging somewhere in the kitchen. You can use the master list to check off or highlight the items you need to buy instead of writing them on multiple lists and risking forgetting something when at the store. Spend a little time writing or typing out a generic list, or print the version at www.JamieNovak.com Try to set up your list by aisle of the store you shop in most often. Check with the store's customer service desk; most stores offer a preprinted directory of the aisles.

You can make this system even more efficient by writing the letter C next to any item you have a coupon for and stapling the coupon directly to the list. That way, you won't forget to bring the coupon to the store, and the C will be your reminder to check that the item you're buying meets the coupon's requirements.

## How can I save time cooking?

Follow these tips:

- Anticipate extra-busy days and plan something quick for them, like sandwiches, pita pizzas, omelets, soup, or grilled quesadillas.

- Make twice as much of whatever you cook and freeze half. It doesn't take much more time or energy to make two batches of lasagna, a bigger pot of chili, or a huge pan of tuna casserole. Later, all you have to do is thaw, heat, and serve.
- Browning ground beef for dinner? Cook extra to use in tacos later that week.
- Baking chicken breasts? Cook a few extra, and cut them up later for a stir-fry with vegetables and brown rice.
- Cook extra rice, put it into a container, and refrigerate or freeze it. On a busy night, microwave it, stirring occasionally, until heated through. Then use as you would fresh.
- Chop a whole onion, even if you only need part of it right now. Store the rest for another meal.
- Grate extra cheese and store it in a resealable plastic bag in the freezer
- Ask trusted friends and family members to recommend time-saving gadgets they themselves find useful.

## My coupon drawer is not working. I spend time clipping coupons but never use them. What can I do?

First, assess whether you have the time and desire to have a coupon drawer. Savings can add up when you use coupons, but if you clip them and never have time to review them before shopping, you might want to stop clipping them altogether.

However, if you are ready to clip and use the coupons, here is a great system. The key is to always have the coupons with you when you need them, and to use them before they expire. Buy a 3 x 5 inch or 4 x 6 inch plastic accordion coupon file. Make sure the size you choose fits inside your handbag or in the console of your car. Keep a coupon slicer in the front slot of the file so it is always handy. This time-saving gadget allows you to simply slice out coupons without wielding a bulky pair of scissors. Label each of the other file slots with broad categories like Clothing, Home, Food, or Restaurants, or with names of the stores you frequent. As you clip the coupons, slip them directly into the accordion file, then place the file back in your bag so you don't leave home without it. As you add new coupons, check whether the ones already there have expired. Immediately throw away any expired coupons.

The next time you make a shopping list, reference your coupon file first. Jot the letter C next to any item on the list for which you have a coupon. Staple the coupons directly to your shopping list or wrap them around the store discount card or your credit card so when you go to pay you'll have them in your hand. This accordion file is also the perfect place to stash store credits, gift cards, or receipts for returns.

### My recipes are everywhere, and I never get around to using them. What are some suggestions?

Designate one place to store recipes. There are a few ways to store recipes easily. You can staple them to index cards and store them by category in an index file box using the tabs. Or, store the recipe cards in a three-ring notebook filled with clear plastic sheet protectors and using the file tabs to categorize the recipes. Instead of printing online recipes, try storing them on the recipe website. Most recipe sites offer an online recipe box. As you try recipes, keep the winners and toss the losers. You might also set criteria for whether to keep a recipe. For example, if a recipe requires too many ingredients or unusual/expensive ingredients, discard it.

### Our leftovers always go bad in the refrigerator because we forget to eat them. How can we avoid this?

Designate one area of your fridge to store all the leftovers, such as the front of the top shelf. That way, they are less likely to get pushed to the back of the fridge and forgotten.

You can also make up plates of leftovers that are easy to reheat or pack leftovers right away for lunches. Another option is to reserve one night of the week as "leftover night" and reheat all the leftover meals. Since this might not be the most popular dinner, find creative ways to enhance the meals, such as transforming leftover baked chicken into a chicken salad sandwich. Finally, place a menu board on the fridge and write down all the leftovers as you put them in the fridge. The menu board can be a piece of paper, a white board, or a chalkboard. Anyone looking for a snack or a meal can read the menu for options.

## What's the best way to identify stuff in the freezer?

Try color-coding items. For example, use containers with red lids for meat, yellow lids for poultry, and green lids for vegetables. You can also opt for a freezer bag, labeling it so you know what's inside. You can also hang a sheet of paper inside a kitchen cupboard to create a perpetual freezer inventory sheet. Write the list in pencil so you can erase or add items easily. Alternatively, slip the inventory sheet in a clear plastic sheet protector or laminate the sheet so you can use a dry-erase marker to erase and add items. On the left-hand side of the sheet in a single column, make an alphabetical list of all the items you usually have in your freezer, by category. For example, under Poultry, list chicken breasts, ground chicken, and turkey breast. Under Ready to Heat, list beef stew and lasagna. Jot down the number you have of each item, even if the number is zero. As you add something to or remove something from the freezer, cross off the original number and write the new one. This way you can always see how many items you have left.

## How long can I freeze food?

Freezing food is a great way to keep whole meals and ingredients on hand. Wrapping food tightly and storing it properly greatly increases its freezer lifespan. Frozen foods remain safe almost indefinitely but won't taste as great when kept longer than noted below:

- Bacon and sausage: 1 to 2 months
- Casseroles: 2 to 3 months
- Egg whites or egg substitutes: 12 months
- Frozen dinners and entrees: 3 to 4 months
- Gravy, meat or poultry: 2 to 3 months
- Ham, hot dogs, and lunchmeats: 1 to 2 months
- Meat, uncooked roasts: 4 to 12 months
- Meat, uncooked steaks or chops: 4 to 12 months
- Meat, uncooked ground: 3 to 4 months
- Meat, cooked: 2 to 3 months
- Poultry, uncooked whole: 12 months
- Poultry, uncooked parts: 9 months
- Poultry, uncooked giblets: 3 to 4 months
- Poultry, cooked: 4 months
- Soups and stews: 2 to 3 months
- Wild game, uncooked: 8 to 12 months

## Is there any way to make kitchen cleanup faster?

The professional chef's tip is to clean as you go. Attend to spills as you cook; most spills clean up faster before they dry. Try filling the sink or a dishpan with soapy water before you begin to cook. Then, add dirty pots and pans to the water so they can soak as you continue to cook. You might also find it helpful to take an extra moment before serving dinner to load the dishwasher. That way, if you delegate the meal cleanup to someone else, you won't have any more dishes to load.

## I can't find things in my refrigerator. What am I doing wrong?

Chances are you're not grouping like items together inside the fridge, so everything is scattered. The best thing to do is to designate certain shelves for certain categories of food. Put all the juice boxes in one area, all the condiments in another, and all the leftovers in yet another area. If you know that everything needed to make a sandwich is in one drawer, then you can pull out the drawer, set it on the countertop, make the sandwich, and put everything back easily. You may have to move some of the refrigerator shelves around. For example, if you want all drinks on the bottom shelf but they're too tall, simply move the shelves. It may take some practice, but once you get the right placement it will work for a long time to come. After a few weeks, everyone will be used to grabbing things from their assigned spots, and finding something in the fridge will be a snap.

## What's the best way to clean the refrigerator?

It's important to clean your refrigerator regularly to eliminate spills and odors. Follow these steps:

1. Turn the temperature-control knob inside the refrigerator to "Off."
2. Take everything out of the refrigerator. If you happen to have a cooler and ice packs handy, you can toss items into the cooler. This is not absolutely necessary, since you'll be quick about getting it back in, but a suggestion for those who may prefer to keep everything cool.
3. Fill the kitchen sink with warm water and a splash of dishsoap.
4. Throw away any food that is moldy, outdated, or otherwise spoiled. I had to mention it, but I think you were one step ahead of me on that one.

5. Take all removable parts out of the refrigerator, including shelves, wire racks, and drawers. Some shelves slide out but are not meant to be removed, so be careful.

6. Wipe down the walls, top, and bottom, along with any shelves that were not removed and the sliders for the shelves and drawers to glide on.

7. Hand wash the shelves, wire racks, and drawers, and then rinse them with warm water. Let the shelves, wire racks, and drawers drain in a dish rack, on paper towels

8. For odor control, use a solution of two tablespoons of baking soda to one quart of warm water to wash the inside of the refrigerator. A solution of one cup of vinegar and one gallon of warm water is also effective. Apply the solution and rinse. Place a box of baking soda in the refrigerator to absorb odors.

9. Replace all shelves, wire racks, and drawers. Measure first! Take the tallest item you store, like a gallon of juice or a pitcher, and adjust your shelving around that. Be sure to line the drawers with paper towels to absorb any messy spills for easier cleanup.

10. Turn the temperature control knob inside the refrigerator back to the recommended setting.

11. Wash the outside of the refrigerator and the gasket (rubber molding around the door) with warm, soapy water. Rinse and wipe dry.

12. Return the food to the refrigerator in an organized fashion. Group similar items together—all the marinades in one spot and all the sandwich-making supplies in another. Remember to wipe off any bottles or jars that are sticky. Place jars that tend to drip in muffin foils to catch any future spills.

## How can I keep my spices organized in the cabinet?

Most people keep all of their spices together. Keeping like items together isn't that simple in this situation. Usually, there are too many spices in one place, and often they don't fit neatly. However, because there are multiple categories of spices, you can still use the like with like theory. Store the spices most often used while baking, like cinnamon and nutmeg, with other baking supplies. If you have any marinating spices, keep them with other marinades or the containers you commonly marinade in. The go-to spices you use weekly, such as garlic powder, should be kept near the stovetop. The remaining spices should now fit in the cabinet without toppling out when you open the door. When storing spices, remember that they do not spoil, but they do lose their strength. Stored in airtight containers, leafy herbs will retain their potency for about two years, ground spices for about three years, and whole spices for about four years.

## Where can I store place mats so they don't jam my drawers or get damaged?

Take advantage of the wasted under-the-shelf space in your kitchen cabinets. You can buy an under-the-shelf basket at most home stores for fewer than ten dollars. The basket attaches to the shelf above it, creating a storage solution above the items on the shelf below. The basket makes it easy to store and retrieve place mats. If you put the place mat basket on the same shelf that holds your everyday plates, you can quickly grab everything you need to set the table.

## I can never find a pot holder when I need one. Any ideas?

First, look at the loops on your pot holders and purchase a few stick-on hooks that will fit into the loops. You'll put the stick-on hooks inside the cabinet door nearest to the stove, staggering them far enough apart so that the pot holders won't overlap. First, however, put the pot holders on the hooks to determine the best placement. If a pot holder is large, the hook should be placed near the center of the door. Otherwise when you try to close the cabinet door, the pot holder will get stuck and the door will not close completely. Make sure that there will be enough room for the door to close completely after you put the pot holder on the hook. If your cabinets have little or no gap between the door and the shelf, pick a spot above or below the shelf so the door can shut.

Store only your most used pot holders on the hooks; don't try to jam every pot holder you own on the hooks. Leave spare pot holders in the pantry. Store holiday pot holders with corresponding holiday decorations so they don't take up valuable space when not in use. If you have decorative pot holders that are not to be used, hang them on a kitchen wall.

## What are some tips for putting away clean dishes faster?

If you store your dishes and cups in cabinets that are far from the dishwasher, move them closer to the dishwasher. Make sure that there is room for the dishes in the cabinet as well. Having to move a stack of small plates to put the larger ones underneath wastes time. If necessary, spend an hour reorganizing the dishes. You don't have to clean out all the cabinets; just make the dishes more accessible. Placing like items together when filling the dishwasher will also make it easier to put them away quickly.

## I need more kitchen cabinet space. What are some suggestions?

Relocate rarely used and excess items so they're not crowding your cabinets. If you have twelve wineglasses in a cabinet but rarely have twelve people over for wine, keep only a few glasses in the cabinet and store the rest. The same holds true for drinking glasses, coffee cups, and other items. By simply removing the excess you can gain a tremendous amount of usable cabinet space. Box up and label the extras, and place them in storage. You can always retrieve them when you have guests over. Another way to free up space is to look at appliances like a waffle iron, sno-cone maker, or fondue set. If you use them occasionally, keep them in storage. If not, share them with friends and neighbors, or donate them to a charitable resale shop.

## Can gadgets make my kitchen more disorganized?

Absolutely. Many gadgets have lots of parts and take more time to clean than they do to use. Plus, you have to remember that you own the gadgets, be able to find them when you need them, and store them when they're not in use. Choose your gadgets wisely, and ruthlessly weed out the ones you already own. Love them or lose them.

## How can I cut down on the time I spend cooking?

Consider joining a cooking club. Cooking clubs are groups of friends and family members who cook bulk meals once a week and share them with other members of the group. They are a huge time—and sanity—saver. You can get a week's worth of meals in exchange for just a few hours of cooking. The ideal group size is six to seven members, though it may take some time to expand your club to this size. But even swapping meals with one other person can cut your meal planning in half. In the beginning, you can swap fewer meals or make two meals each to share. Each member cooks a meal in bulk and portions it into storage containers, with the name of the dish and cooking instructions attached. Meals can be frozen, or just refrigerated and used in the next few days. Then the meals are swapped. Each member of the club gets one of each meal for the week. You can deliver the meals to other group members, or everyone can meet in a central location for the swap.

# *Chapter 8*  KIDS

- How can I get my kids to clean up their toys when I ask them to?
- What can I do with the random items my kids leave around the house?
- When should I start to involve my children in the organizing process?
- How can I get my child to follow through on my request to put away her things?
- Is a family calendar a good idea?
- What belongs on my child's checklist?
- When I drop my child off for a birthday party or a playdate, I scribble notes for the other parent, like my child's allergies and my cell phone number. There has to be a better way. Any suggestions?
- What can I do to stop misplacing library books?
- How can I organize my home to help give my child a good start to the school year?
- We misplace our children's homework that's in progress and not due until later in the week. Where should we store it so we can find it again?
- What steps should I take to organize our playroom?
- What are the best storage solutions for toys?
- How can I prevent my kids' toys from ending up in our living space? We don't have a playroom.
- How should I store stuffed animals?
- My child's messy room: leave it or clean it?
- How can I get my kids to take their stuff with them when they get out of the car?
- What's the best way to store my child's artwork?
- How can I get my child to stop throwing all the toys in one large container?
- What's the best way to organize important family information?
- What can I do to help mornings run more smoothly?
- How can we make the evening routine easier?

## How can I get my kids to clean up their toys when I ask them to?

Try the "Saturday Box" exercise. Warn your kids that they have ten minutes to clean up their toys. You might want to set a timer to help keep them on track. When the ten minutes are up, don't nag your kids about the toys that are still left out. Instead, simply confiscate those toys and place them in a box called the Saturday Box. On Saturday, and not a moment before, release the items from the box to the children. Typically, you'll get 100 percent compliance from kids after the first time their toys are put into the box and left there until the next Saturday.

## What can I do with the random items my kids leave around the house?

Set up a lost and found container. This system can work as well in your home as it does in schools and libraries. Instead of having to track down the owner or to put the item away yourself, simply toss it into the lost and found container. When the owner comes looking for the item, direct him or her to the lost and found. Eventually, your child will get into the habit of checking lost and found without needing to ask you.

To get started, designate one spot in your home that's easily accessible to every member of the family and make it the lost and found. Some ideas include a kitchen drawer, a living room ottoman with a lid that lifts up for storage inside, or a decorative basket with a lid that slides under a side table in the hallway. Toss any stray items around your home into this container. For example, a black cord left on your kitchen counter, a battery left on the dining room table, a single toy left on the living room chair, or a T-shirt left on the floor.

## When should I start to involve my children in the organizing process?

Involve your children from day one, or almost day one. Children tend to imitate their parents, learning what they see. Even before they can pick up and put away items themselves, they will be observing your organizing habits, so the first step is to be a good example for your child. When your child can walk, he can begin to help organize. Maybe he can walk to a container to put a ball away while you cheer, teaching him to correlate putting things away with your being pleased. If the stack rings toy is out and he wants to bring out the blocks, insist on putting away one toy before getting another. To encourage putting toys where they belong, tape a photo to the inside bottom of containers that shows which items belong inside. If your kids are past the toddler stage, it's not too late to instill some of these habits. You'll simply need to talk about the new household guidelines and institute one at a time so as not to overwhelm your kids.

## How can I get my child to follow through on my request to put away her things?

Keep it simple. List one or two tasks at a time instead of giving your child a long list of things to do. Use as few words as possible for your request and make sure your expectations are clear. Instead of saying, "I've asked you a million times not to make a mess in your room," say something like, "By Sunday bedtime I need this room to be clean so we can have an organized school week." Don't nag your child on Sunday afternoon or warn her that she only has four hours left. Try giving an incentive. Say something like, "As soon as your toys are put away we can go outside to play." You can also try setting consequences for not following through on a request. Ask your child to help determine the consequence; usually, kids come up with something worse than a parent would have picked anyway. Always recognize and celebrate successes. Say, "Wow, you did a great job putting that away! I'm so proud of you."

## Is a family calendar a good idea?

A family calendar isn't just a good idea, it's a must. It helps keep your life in order while showing your children how to manage time. The best spot for the family calendar is in the kitchen, on the front or side of the refrigerator, inside the pantry door, or on a wall. Assign a different color pen to each family member and keep the pens near the calendar. Write on the calendar events, appointments, and deadlines. If a child has a party to attend, write the party time and address on the calendar in that child's color. If a child has a school spirit day, use the appropriate color of pen to make a note on the calendar that he or she needs to wear the T-shirt with the school logo on it. And if one child has a book report due, make a note of the deadline on the calendar in that child's color. To take planning to the next level, note the deadline as well as a reminder a week or two in advance. For example, the weekend before the birthday party, make a note to buy the gift when you're out running errands. Make a note on the laundry day before school spirit day to wash the logo T-shirt. Jot down a similar advance note for the book report so your child doesn't leave it for the night before it's due. Finally, remember that a family calendar system will only work if you check the calendar regularly.

## What belongs on my child's checklist?

A checklist for your child can serve as a visual reminder of the tasks he or she needs to complete before leaving for school. Make a chart using pictures and/or words, of your child performing a task like brushing his teeth or putting on his shoes. Use a few pictures in a row to make a visual checklist for the task, and hang it on the back of the bathroom or bedroom door so your child can follow it.

## When I drop my child off for a birthday party or a playdate, I scribble notes for the other parent, like my child's allergies and my cell phone number. There has to be a better way. Any suggestions?

Create business cards on your home computer that list your contact information and any pertinent information about your children, so that when you drop your child off for a playdate you can simply hand the card to the parent.

## What can I do to stop misplacing library books?

Pick a single location to store all borrowed items, like movies and library books. By having a dedicated "borrowed basket" you can easily find a library book on the day it is due. No more scouring the bookshelves to locate it or finding it months later when you clean.

## How can I organize my home to help give my child a good start to the school year?

Set up a School Station in your home a few weeks before school begins. The end of summer is a perfect time to create this simple organization system for your home and life.

Here's how to set up the station:

- Start with a bookshelf. Using a slim, floor-to-ceiling bookshelf is a good way to take advantage of vertical space without taking up too much floor space. Try to place the bookshelf nearest the door used most often, so family members can grab what they need on the way out and easily place items there when they return. If you don't have a spare bookshelf, search for a used one at www.Freecycle.org or www.CraigsList.com, or buy an affordable new one If there's not enough space near the door, consider clearing out the hall closet and sliding the bookshelf inside.

- If two people will be sharing the station, divide the shelves with a vertical strip of tape. You can also opt to paint the shelves two different colors.
- Screw in hooks or stick removable hooks to the side of the shelves (lower for small children) for jackets, hats, and umbrellas.
- Cut a hole in the back of the shelf and run an extension cord through as the place to plug in your cell phone, PDA, iPod, and other electronics. Tape down the cord to keep it from slipping away.
- Slide a milk crate onto the bottom shelf for shoes and backpacks or briefcases.
- Label one shelf as "outgoing" for all the items ready to leave the house, such as bills to mail.
- Place a jar on one shelf for lunch money, toll change, or lunch tickets.
- Add trays or boxes, one labeled "in" and one labeled "out" for permission slips, or incoming and outgoing mail.
- Consider sticking a dry-erase board to one side of the bookshelf for daily notes or to write out a weekly schedule. If you prefer a chalkboard, you can use chalkboard paint to paint the side of the bookshelf.

## We misplace my children's homework that's in progress and not due until later in the week. Where should we store it so we can find it again?

Give each child a colorful two-pocket file folder. Slide the homework pages into one of the pockets and store the folders standing up on the countertop between the sugar and flour canisters. The homework folder will act as a visual reminder and will always be easy to locate.

## What steps should I take to organize our playroom?

Set your kitchen timer for eighteen minutes and work on the playroom once a day, in eighteen-minute blocks of time, until it's organized. Follow these three steps:

1.  **Sort the toys into piles of like with like.**
    Separate all the toys into categories, grouping like items together. Building blocks, tools, dolls, books, crafts, coloring, action figures, puzzles, electronics, play food, musical instruments, stuffed animals, dress-up, trains and cars, and cooking items each get their own pile. Remove the toys that will be played with in other areas of the home besides the playroom. For example, you may want to keep books and stuffed animals in the bedroom, or ride-on toys and balls in the garage for outside play. Once you've decided which toys will stay in the playroom, then you know how many functions the room needs to serve. For example, you may have a crafts and coloring area, a pretend play space, and a train table. Dividing up the room and designating an area for each type of play helps to contain the mess as well as make it easier to clean.

2.  **Put away only what the kids use and love, donating or throwing away the rest.**
    Look at each pile of toys. Discard broken toys, part with excess toys, and donate or pass along toys your kids no longer use. Remember that children's playing habits and toy preferences change. If you're not sure whether your child is

ready to part with a toy, use the box it, date it, tape it, toss it method (see page 57). Next, plan how you'll store the toys that will stay in the playroom.

Consider the size and measurements of the toys in each category. For example, stack the coloring books and measure the height and width of the largest book. That way, you can find or buy a container that will fit them all. See the following question for more tips on storing toys. Once all the toys are contained, the next step is to keep them that way so all of your hard work doesn't go down the drain.

3.  **Maintain the space using new guidelines.**
    Get your children involved in keeping the space organized. They can help you come up with new rules for how to play with toys in your home. Post the new rules in the playroom to help children remember them.

Here are some suggestions for rules:
- You can have only two toys out at a time.
- Clean up before leaving the playroom.
- Playdates help clean up ten minutes before they go home.
- Once a crayon is only an inch long, throw it away.
- Throw away markers that don't have lids.
- Give five toys to a charity each month.
- When we get a new toy, the old version goes to a new home.
- Every evening we tidy up for five minutes.

## What are the best storage solutions for toys?

If your family room and playroom are combined, use creative storage solutions such as a storage ottoman. Maximize the room's space by going vertical, using floor-to-ceiling bookshelves instead of short, horizontal ones that attract clutter. Other great storage options are ziplock bags, perfect for doll accessories or game cords. Rolling bins are another great option. They allow the children to roll toys to where they want to play. Having the containers right next to the play area also makes cleanup a snap. Opt for shallow bins instead of deeper bins for storage. It's much easier to find things in shallow bins, and they're not as heavy to move. Children usually have a difficult time with lids, so choose open bins or tubs for the toys they use often. Have the children help you label the bins and containers. Each label can include the name and then a picture of what is inside. To store items like action figures and doll accessories, hang a plastic over-the-door shoe holder on the back of the playroom door. Place a second over-the-door shoe holder lower on the door for all the items smaller children can access without supervision. Keep puzzles and all their pieces together by color-coding them. Using a different color or marker for each puzzle, place a dot on the back of each puzzle piece and on the back of the board itself. You'll never mix up puzzle pieces again. Designate one shelf or basket for borrowed items like library books. Remember to leave room to grow. Your children are bound to get more toys. Empty space is a good thing, so don't feel like you have to fill every container and space with toys.

## How can I prevent my kids' toys from ending up in our living space? We don't have a playroom.

It's virtually impossible to prevent your children from playing in one of the most centrally located rooms of your home, especially if you don't have dedicated space for toys. A better solution is figuring out a way to blend the toys into your home's decor. First, decide which toys belong in which areas of the house. Stuffed animals might be bedroom toys, clay might be a kitchen toy for easy cleanup, and board games and the play kitchen might be family room toys. Then plan ways to store the toys in those areas. Board games can be placed in a shallow bin and slid under the couch. Sometimes the drawers of a coffee table are wide enough for the boxes to fit. Another storage option is an ottoman whose lid lifts up for storage. Baskets slid under end tables or the coffee table are also great ways to conceal clutter. The play kitchen, however, can be a different story; large primary- or pastel-colored toys rarely complement home decor. Hide it as well as possible. Depending on the setup of your room, you might be able to pull the couch away from a wall to make a narrow play area for the kitchen.

## How should I store stuffed animals?

Before storing stuffed animals, try to pare down the collection. If you are unsure about which ones to part with, try boxing up the "maybes" and putting them away for a few months. If your children don't miss them, then the entire box can be donated or tossed. Although some charities don't accept stuffed toys, there are others that do. Once you've decided which stuffed animals to keep, store them in a toy hammock that attaches to a corner wall. A large bin also can house the stuffed animals. Another option is bungee cords. Attach them to the wall and then slip in an arm or leg of a stuffed animal to hold it in place.

## My child's messy room: leave it or clean it?

A team effort, at least in the beginning, is probably the best way to deal with a child's messy room. Setting your child up for lifelong success in this area is important. They are never too young, and it is never too late to start.

1.  Make space to organize. Before you can assign the job, you have to be sure the job can actually be done. Otherwise, you

might be asking for something that cannot be accomplished. Maybe the storage bin is too heavy for your child to move, the dresser drawer has a broken rail, or the hanging rod in the closet is too full to fit another hanger. First ask your child to show you how she does it. Maybe it's not that she doesn't want to; maybe it's that she can't.

2. Be realistic and specific. Be realistic in what you are asking to be done. "Clean your room" might be too overwhelming, while "Put the art supplies in the red box" might not.

3. Ask for help. Enlist your child's assistance in selecting colored bins and containers from the store. When your child is involved in the process, he or she has more at stake to make the solution work.

4. Make it fun. Time it Race it! Play music! Hide a treasure to find while cleaning! Make it a game! Join in; by making it fun, you remove the stress and the job becomes easier.

5. Use rewards. Using rewards as motivators can work wonders. Rewards help your child understand the importance of a clean space. Promising to do something fun after your child's room is organized shows your child that there are real benefits to having a clean space.

## How can I get my kids to take their stuff with them when they get out of the car?

A travel bag might be just the answer. Give each child a single bag, like a tote or small backpack. This is the bag they'll pack before going in the car, and the bag they'll bring out of the car. Also keep a trash bag in the car within children's reach and have them grab it when leaving the car.

## What's the best way to store my child's artwork?

Make a treasure box where you can store all of your child's important papers. Write your child's name and the school year on the outside edge, and then fill the box with all the treasures they create. Keep in mind that some children are more prolific than others, so the pile may need some culling. Save only the very best or the firsts, such as the first time a child printed his name or the first A received on a test. If you save everything, the good stuff will get lost among the mess. Consider letting your child help to decide what makes the cut. This will teach your child that he can't save everything. If your child seems disappointed to let go of some artwork, try using it as wrapping paper on gifts or as a place mat at dinnertime. You can also mail your child's artwork to family members or use it in photo albums or scrapbooks.

## How can I get my child to stop throwing all the toys in one large container?

Cleaning up isn't always easy, and sometimes kids just don't know what to do. So they either don't do anything at all, or they pile everything all in one place. If your child puts everything in one container, it might mean that they don't have proper storage options. Their storage spots might be inconvenient or overcrowded. Instead of offering your child a large bin for storage, try a bunch of smaller containers clearly labeled with pictures and words. That way your child will know what goes where. You might opt to leave off the lids, as they make it more difficult to toss items inside. Bins on rolling casters are ideal since they can be wheeled to the play area and wheeled back.

## What's the best way to organize important family information?

Keep a three-ring binder in your kitchen that will serve as a family notebook. Store important family papers and essential information inside the binder. Use three-ring tabbed dividers to clearly label the sections. Here are examples of tabs to include:

- Contact information (cell phone numbers, emergency numbers, numbers of nearby friends and neighbors who can help in an emergency)
- Medical information (each child's medications and dosages; doctor's names, numbers, and addresses; maps to doctor offices and the closest hospital)
- Household information (which remote control turns on the TV versus which one is used for the cable box and the game systems)
- List of babysitters
- Playdates' contact information and directions to their homes
- School menus and lunch tickets
- Child's sporting, scouting, and other extracurricular activity schedules
- Party invitations

## What can I do to help mornings run more smoothly?

Here are twenty tips to restore sanity to your morning:

1. If you have more than one child, stagger their wake-up times so you have time to assist the ones who need your help.
2. Place your alarm clock across the room so you're forced to get out of bed to turn it off. This will lessen your chances of hitting the snooze button and running late.
3. Wear a watch set to the correct time while getting ready, and consider placing a small clock in the bathroom. You can easily lose track of time while fixing your hair.
4. Hang a mirror outside your bathroom. Competition for the bathroom is usually just for the mirror.

5. Designate one area of your calendar, to-do list, or PDA for morning tasks so you can see them at a glance without previewing the entire day.

6. Keep your keys on a stretch-coiled bracelet so your hands are free to carry things (and possibly children) as you leave the house.

7. Create an area in your entryway (nearest the door you use most often) for everyday life accessories like keys, cell phone and charger, and bills to be mailed. An over-the-door clear plastic holder is an ideal storage spot for these items. Set aside lower pockets for small children's things so they can get their own belongings.

8. Fill a weekly or monthly pillbox with the day's vitamins and medications instead of unscrewing multiple bottles each morning.

9. Fill the coffeemaker in the evening and set the time to start brewing first thing in the morning. If your coffeemaker doesn't have a timer, use a vacation timer. Simply plug the coffeemaker into the vacation timer before you plug it into the wall, and it will flip on the coffeemaker at the time you set.

10. Dedicate a spot in your kitchen for a coffee/tea station and stock it with a few mugs, sugar, spoons, tea bags, and so on. You won't have to open and close multiple cabinets to get your morning brew.

11. Set a timer to go off ten minutes before you need to leave the house as a gentle reminder.

12. Eliminate as many interruptions as possible. For example, if your child always asks you for a juice box from the top shelf of the fridge, simply move the juice boxes down a few shelves so she can help herself.

13. Screen morning phone calls, allowing non-urgent calls to go to voice mail to be returned at a less hectic time of the day.
14. Make it a house rule that there is no TV, computer games, or phone until everyone is ready.
15. Use colored tote bags to store equipment—one bag per activity. For example, a blue bag for scouting and a red bag for ballet. That way you can easily grab the right bag on the right day without having to empty and refill a single bag.
16. Make lunches and pack backpacks while making dinner the night before. You'll have one cleanup instead of two, plus you can fill out important forms like permission slips while you're waiting for the pasta to boil.
17. If you need to remember to take a refrigerated item, like a packed lunch, with you, put your keys with the item. If you have cupcakes for the bake sale in the fridge, place your keys on top, so you can't leave without them.
18. Whenever possible, make breakfast ahead of time. If you make pancakes on a Sunday, make extra and freeze them so you can reheat them in the microwave on a busy morning.
19. Write out simple checklists for every member of the family with the top five tasks that need to be completed during his or her morning routine (e.g., brush teeth, bring hair clips and brush to Mom, etc.). Hang the checklists on the bathroom doorknob (a central location, since everyone visits the bathroom daily).
20. Dedicate a spot near the door you use most often as the leaving zone. Place items you need to leave with there. Having your purse, umbrella, bills to be mailed, and all those last-minute-items in the leaving zone lessens the chance that you'll leave without them.

## How can we make the evening routine easier?

Here are six ways to make your evening routine easier:

1.  Instead of buying take-out dinners on busy evenings, cook a frozen food item or serve a ready-made dish from the grocery store that you bought during your regular weekly shopping trip.
2.  Allow time for you and family members to transition from a busy day to a relaxed evening.
3.  Play relaxing music instead of turning on the television.
4.  Lower the lights and light some candles to set a relaxing mood.
5.  Reserve one evening a week for family time, free from outside activities.
6.  Have scheduled homework time for your child, possibly right after dinner but before dessert. That means your child will be well fed and looking forward to wrapping up the homework so he or she can get a treat.

*Chapter 9*

# OUT-OF-THE-ORDINARY TIMES

- How can I make holiday time better organized?
- Guests are on the way and I feel unprepared. What can I do to get ready?
- I'd like to mail a family photo with our holiday cards this year. How can I make sure it gets done?
- How can I make gift wrapping easier?
- How can I organize a space for overnight guests?
- How can I simplify the process of shopping for gifts?
- How can I host a better Thanksgiving meal?
- How can I organize a college search for my child?
- What's the best way to organize a party?
- What's the best way to quickly clean before company arrives?
- What's the best way to estimate how much food I'll need per person when entertaining?
- What's the best way to prepare to move to a new home?
- What's the easiest way to pack my belongings for a move?
- How can I make the first few days in a new home easier?
- What's the best way to organize my home for an open house?
- What's the easiest way to find a reliable handyman?
- After a move, how can I unpack in an organized manner?
- I agreed to help my parent downsize thirty years of belongings to move to an assisted living facility. Where should we start?
- I'd like to organize an emergency kit. What belongs inside?
- What belongs in a basic first-aid kit?

## How can I make holiday time better organized?

Create a holiday binder, an organizing tool that you'll use for years to come. To make your holiday binder, use a one-inch, three-ring binder filled with three-hole-punched sheet protectors, lined notepaper, and a three-hole-punched pencil pouch. You also might want to include a few three-hole-punched slash pockets. Use the binder to house menu ideas, guest lists, shopping lists, gift ideas, and more. Slip clipped recipes, decorating ideas, and other notes from magazines or printed from websites into the sheet protectors. Make notes about what gifts you bought people, your budget, how you arranged your furniture so it all fit, and other things you'll want to remember for next year. Don't forget to include trips to take, fun projects to do, and places to visit during the holiday season. Keep pens in the pouch and store the binder with fall decorations so you can start using it before the next holiday season.

## Guests are on the way and I feel unprepared. What can I do to get ready?

Here are some helpful tips:

- Avoid scooping papers into a bag or basket and hiding them in a closet when people are coming over. Instead, scoop up the piles of paper and place them on your bed. Then you'll at least be forced to deal with them before you go to sleep that night.
- When people pop by unannounced, work on the visible surfaces only. If guests are about to arrive, just touch up the surfaces. Your guests won't inspect the insides of your closets, so don't worry about them.
- If you're short on space, disguise the clutter. You can stow things under a table and then throw a floor-length tablecloth over the table to hide everything.

- When you're hosting a party, contain the party to the living space of your home. There is no need for visitors to take a full house tour. Clear space in the closet for coats by simply taking out some of your stuff and placing it on your bed, possibly using the bedspread as disguise.
- Have some stain remover on hand for spills on your carpet and on guests' clothing.
- Stash extra paper products in a visible place like a basket on the bathroom floor with spare hand towels and a scented candle.
- The best idea is to just step back, stop worrying, and relax. Your guests understand—they have clutter in their lives, too. Enjoy the moment and forget about the clutter.

## I'd like to mail a family photo with our holiday cards this year. How can I make sure it gets done?

Instead of stressing over getting everyone together for a family portrait during the busiest time of the year, create a unique and memorable holiday card that includes various photographs from the past year, along with your children's artwork and other treasures. Collect these items, arrange them on a piece of paper, and make color photocopies to send as the card.

To automate the addressing of the envelopes, put your holiday card list in an electronic spreadsheet and print the addresses directly on the envelopes. Or use an online service that allows you to upload your address list and sends the cards for you.

## How can I make gift wrapping easier?

Create a gift-wrapping caddy. Fill a bucket, basket, or box with the necessary supplies, including gift wrap, scissors, and tape. During busy gift-wrapping times designate one area as "gift wrap central" where you'll keep all the supplies. Keep bows and embellishments in one place. (To keep ribbons untangled, hang a clear plastic over-the-door shoe holder in the wrapping area. Place one type of ribbon in each slot and punch a small hole to thread the ribbon through.) During busy times like the Christmas holiday, multitask by hosting a gift wrap party. Invite friends, socialize, and share gift-wrapping ideas while you work.

## How can I organize a space for overnight guests?

Doing a few simple things can really make your guests feel welcome. Place sample sizes of lotions and shampoos in a decorative basket on the bathroom vanity with a sign that says "Help yourself." Place a lamp and alarm at the bedside along with an extra comforter. You can even create a personal minibar for your guests with glasses, napkins, drinks, an ice bucket, and packages of snacks. Leave reading material on the nightstand with a note that says, "Please take it with you if you're not done by the time you leave." Fresh flowers and a mint on the pillow show your guests that you're glad they're visiting. When your guests have left, pop all the supplies into a box and clearly label it so the next time you have guests you have everything at hand.

## How can I simplify the process of shopping for gifts?

Choose a theme for all of your gifts to make gift buying easier. For example, your theme for holiday gifts one year can be movie night. That means you give everyone a DVD, popcorn, a box of candy, and a throw blanket to curl up with. Another theme could be ice cream. Everyone on your list gets an ice-cream maker and fun sundae bowls with delicious toppings. Another option is consumable gifts such as gift certificates or gift cards. Gift certificates are easy on you as the shopper and on the recipient since you're giving an experience and memory rather than more stuff. Gift certificates for spa services, restaurants, theater, tickets or a museum trip make nice gifts. You also can give something to complement the monetary gift, like a bottle of wine with a restaurant gift certificate or opera glasses with a gift certificate for theater tickets.

## How can I host a better Thanksgiving meal?

Make a master plan and save it so you can use it from year to year. Here's the one I've used for years (feel free to personalize it with your own notes):

### *Early November*

- Plan your menu.
- Invite your guests.
- Keep track of who is bringing what on your menu.
- Make shopping list of perishables and nonperishables. Don't forget to include film, batteries, and beverages.
- If you're ordering a fresh turkey, do it now.
- Make a Thanksgiving to-do list, listing all the little things you need to do prior to Thanksgiving. Be sure to schedule time for each chore and indicate who will take care of that chore. If you're inviting overnight guests, now is the time to clear out the guest room.
- If you use floral centerpieces, order them now, or schedule time to make a simple one.

### *Two weeks ahead*

- Check all serving dishes, flatware, and glassware.
- Shop for any paper goods you need for the event.
- Make sure you have enough tables and chairs for your guests.
- Take an inventory of your tablecloths and napkins.
- If any of your items need to be cleaned, do it now.

- Clean your refrigerator to make room for your Thanksgiving items.
- Shop for nonperishable groceries on your shopping list.
- Plan and make decorations.

### One week ahead
- Plan seating arrangements.
- Review your recipes.
- Prepare cooking schedule.
- Check thawing time for frozen turkey.

### Four days ahead
- Start defrosting the frozen turkey in your refrigerator.
- Save money on ice—start making your own ice cubes now. When frozen, dump them in a freezer bag.

### Two days ahead
- Chill beverages.
- Shop for perishable items.
- Set out bread for homemade stuffing.
- Make cranberry sauce.
- Fill salt and pepper shakers and butter dishes.
- Be sure your home is clean.

### One day ahead
- Peel potatoes and place in a pot of cold water. Keep in refrigerator.
- Clean vegetables and refrigerate.
- Make all dishes that can be prepared ahead. Don't forget the pies.
- Check your bathrooms. Be sure to have extra toilet paper and hand towels available.
- Put up decorations.

- Prepare stuffing.
- Do spot cleaning of the rooms that will be used.
- Let your family set the table in the evening.
- Make the side dishes that can be baked ahead of time.

### *Thanksgiving Day*
- Remove turkey from the refrigerator for one to two hours. Add stuffing.
- Preheat oven.
- Put turkey in oven and baste every half hour.
- Prepare coffee and brew twenty minutes before serving.
- Keep the turkey covered and let it rest for about twenty minutes before slicing.
- Microwave food to quickly reheat if all the burners of the stove are occupied.
- Make gravy and last-minute vegetables.
- Set out refrigerated dishes.
- Heat bread or rolls as needed.
- Remove stuffing from turkey.
- Carve turkey.

One way to plan the cooking you need to do on Thanksgiving Day is to figure out what time you'll be dining and work backward, so your to-do list will include times to start cooking dishes based on how long they take to cook. If a casserole needs thirty minutes in the oven and you'll be eating at 2:00, then it has to go in the oven at 1:30.

## How can I organize a college search for my child?
Set up a travel file box to store all the college search and application material. Use a plastic hanging file box with a lid, available at office supply stores for under $20. Fill the box with about fifteen hanging

file folders and label one file for each section of the country (East, West, Midwest, and Central). Also make files for scholarships, financial aid, and so on. As college brochures arrive, pop them into the correct file folder based on the school's geographic location. As you start to narrow the search, remove and recycle the brochures from the schools that are not in the running. Whenever you visit a school, keep the file box in the car with you so all the information you need is at your fingertips.

## What's the best way to organize a party?

Before another year goes by without planning a get-together, follow these simple steps to plan a party with ease:

1. Use a file folder or three-ring binder as a single place to collect all your ideas. This is an important first step that makes the rest of the planning much easier.
2. Pull out your calendar and pick a date for the party. Work backward to determine the date you need to send the invitations. (Email invitations from a place like www.evite.com are acceptable and preferred by many.)
3. Choose a theme, which makes planning a lot easier. Once you know your party's theme and the colors, you'll have fewer decisions to make.
4. Collect party items as you come across them and store them in a single box or container. Your year-round box might include items like plastic ware, disposable camera, decorations, and other items, and you can add season-specific items like citronella candles, barbecue lighter, and sunscreen, for example, for a summer event.
5. Make a list of those you want to invite.
6. Start collecting recipes and menu ideas.

7. Send the invitations four to six weeks in advance and track the regrets.
8. Speed clean. (See next question for a speed-cleaning routine.)
9. Make the final preparations: put out the serving platters, check the batteries in your camera, etc.
10. Then enjoy the day!

Once the party is over, take a few moments to make notes in your party binder. Note things like how much food was consumed, if you needed more or less, if some things were a huge hit and others not so much. If you arranged your furniture in a way that really worked, note that and any other helpful tips you want to remember for next time. Then tuck your party binder into a box with any remaining party supplies. Clearly label the box so you can find everything you need next time.

## What's the best way to quickly clean before company arrives?

You'll need fifteen minutes for this speed-clean routine. Start before guests arrive, or have someone show them around the outside of your home while you clean up inside.

What you need:

- 15 minutes
- Lint roller
- Laundry basket or empty box
- Empty garbage bag or container
- Two rags, one damp and one dry
- Room freshener, scented candle, etc.
- Fresh flowers or holiday centerpiece
- Background music

- A basket with sample/trial-size product, and a handwritten sign that says "Help yourself" (optional)

## Step 1

Go into the living room and straighten the magazine pile. Use the damp rag to wipe down surfaces like picture frames and end tables. Use a lint roller on the couch and to spot touch the rug in traffic areas or where pets sleep. Toss piles of unsorted stuff like mail and toys in the box or laundry basket. Collect any stray dishes or anything else that belongs in the kitchen.

## Step 2

Go to the kitchen and put the stray dishes you picked up into the dishwasher. Collect piles of mail, toys, and other things to be dealt with later and place them in the box or laundry basket.

## Step 3

While still in the kitchen, wipe down the countertop and use lint roller on any fabric chairs.

## Step 4

Stop in the dining room, and put the flowers or centerpiece on the table. Collect any other items that have been left out and place them in the laundry basket or box (by this time you may need a second box or basket).

## Step 5

On your way to the bathroom, take laundry basket or box to your bedroom and place it on your bed to be dealt with later.

### Step 6

Spot clean the bathroom and refill paper products. If you have time, put out a small basket with unused trial or sample sizes of lotions and other things for guests to use (and, hopefully, take with them).

### Step 7

Take out the trash and take a final walk through the rooms guests will see. There's no reason to give them a full house tour.

### Last step

Light the candle or spritz the room freshener, turn on the music and open the door to let your guests in.

## What's the best way to estimate how much food I'll need per person when entertaining?

To help organize your event, here are the recommendations from expert party planners about how much to have on hand for your event:

### Hors d'oeuvres
- Six bites when preceding a meal
- Four to six bites per hour when hors d'oeuvres are the meal
- The longer your party and the larger your guest list, the greater the number of hors d'oeuvres selections you should offer.

### The main meal
- Poultry, meat or fish: 8 ounces when you have one main dish, 6 ounces when you offer two or more main courses
- Rice, grains: 1.5 ounces as a side dish, 2 ounces in a main dish such as risotto
- Potatoes: 5 ounces

- Vegetables: 4 ounces
- Beans: 2 ounces as a side dish
- Pasta: 2 ounces for a side dish, 3 ounces for a first course, 4 ounces for a main dish
- Green salad: 1 ounce

### Desserts
- One slice cake, tart, or pastry
- Four ounces creamy dessert such as pudding
- Five ounces ice cream
- When serving two of the above, reduce each by a little less than half.

### Other great ideas
- Label the food on the table; for example, toothpicks in the cheese wedge with a label as to what type.
- Photocopy the recipes and place them out for those who might want them.
- For a barbecue, place condiments directly into a muffin pan instead of using messy bottles.

## What's the best way to prepare to move to a new home?

Relocating is a stressful event; in fact, it rates as one of the top five stressors in people's lives. If you're slightly panicked, that's completely normal. Before your move begins, make a moving binder to keep all the documents related to the move; all the mail that arrives that will need a change of address; business cards; movers' estimates; and other important notes and papers. Use a brightly colored three-ring notebook and put in some folders, paper, clear plastic sheet protectors, and a pencil pouch. Also in advance of your move, start collecting boxes. Most local grocery stores will give you the boxes if you ask for them. The boxes that egg cartons are packed in tend to be the best for packing. Or, consider boxes from U-Haul's box exchange program, where you can pick up boxes from someone else who recently moved at no charge.

Give away any large furniture that you're not taking to the new home. Getting that out of the way early can open a lot of space to maneuver while packing boxes. Designate one place in the house for all the packed moving boxes. Make a moving supplies area. It can be a large basket where you keep tape, scissors, markers, and all the other supplies you might need. As you pack, it can be helpful to wear an apron with pockets; that way you'll always have tape, scissors, and markers on hand. The goal is to pack an entire area before moving on to another area.

The rest of the job is straightforward packing, but it can become emotional. You might feel joyful thinking of past events in your home and sad to say good-bye. To keep your emotions from slowing you down, be sure to rest up before packing, and to eat well and drink plenty of water both before and during the job. Enlist as much help as possible. Unpaid help, like family and friends, is usually preferred. However, you can usually give more direction to paid helpers. Do whatever works best for you.

## What's the easiest way to pack my belongings for a move?

First, pare down your belongings to only the items you use and love. In other words, pack only the stuff you think is worthwhile to move. Donate unused or unwanted items to charity. Choose a charity that picks up donations, and keep their number in your moving notebook. You can call the charity several times for pickups; you don't need to gather everything to give them at once. Create a "maybe box" for all the items you might let go of eventually. Move them to the new home, and if you don't unpack that box within six months, discard it or donate it (without opening it).

Consider having a moving party. Invite friends and family to bring boxes and help you pack. You supply the pizza and drinks, put on music, and everyone packs the night away. Pack like with like, and make the boxes manageable in size and weight. Paper is heavier than you think. Label everything, and label all sides of boxes. When boxes are stacked you can't see some of the sides. Do a little packing each day; you don't have to wait for large chunks of time to pack. By adding even a few pieces to a box a few times a day, entire rooms can be packed in increments. Pack one bag of the essentials so when you get to the new house you don't have to open boxes to find toilet paper or a cup. Include bath towels, paper products, glasses, sheets, and any medication or vitamins. Take a photo of the outside of your house before you leave to preserve the memory.

## How can I make the first few days in a new home easier?

Create a moving survival box. Pack one bag of the essentials so when you get to the new house you don't have to open boxes to find paper towels or a cup. Here are the suggested items:

- Alarm clock
- Bath towels
- Bed linens
- Change of clothes
- Cleaning supplies
- Coffeemaker and mugs
- Corded phone (the battery in the cordless may need time to recharge)

- Disposable window coverings
- Eating and cooking utensils
- Emergency contact numbers
- First-aid kit
- Flashlight
- Food take-out menus
- Medication and vitamins
- Mirror
- Night-lights
- Paper products
- Personal items (soap, toothbrush, glasses, contact lens solution, etc.)
- Pet food and water dish
- Tool kit
- Trash bags
- Water and ice (pack the ice in a cooler the day of the move)

## What's the best way to organize my home for an open house?

First, let's be clear on the objective: to make your home look as spacious and inviting as possible so the potential buyer can imagine happily living there. This translates to a quicker sale and most likely a higher sale price. No matter how cute your children are, photographs of them on the walls is distracting, and no matter how proud you are of your teacup collection, a bunch of teacups collecting dust in a curio cabinet is not the best way to showcase your home. Follow these tips instead:

### *Preparation*
- Walk through your home with a trusted friend, and ask him or her to critique the space.
- Clean windows, carpets, walls, bathrooms, sinks, and more. If it can't be cleaned, replace it.

- Pack away throw rugs; they give the impression you're trying to cover something up.
- Pack away collectibles and photos. Home buyers need to be able to imagine their photos in the home.
- Find out if there are other houses for sale in the area and go to their open houses to get ideas of what works and what doesn't.
- Remember that the more you organize and pack now, the less you'll have to do when the house sells.
- Take down personal artwork and photographs. Rearrange other pieces to give a more open feel to the walls. Patch and paint if necessary.

### Day of open house and showing tips
- Box up items you use every day, like the toaster or kids' toys, then tuck them out of sight. When the showing is over, bring them back out until next time.
- Replace everyday towels in the bathroom with fluffy, clean spa towels, and remove them when the showing is over.
- Turn on all lights and lamps.
- Have a nice scent in the air; use scented candles or an unobtrusive air freshener
- Have a pleasant FM radio station on during viewings.

### Outside the home
- Survey the outside of the home. Remove all garbage cans, wrap up garden hoses, and remove all extra stuff. If you need help, call 1-800-got-junk for removal at a fee.
- Prune the plants or shrubs around your home so they aren't blocking windows. Remove dead plants, and then weed and mulch all planting areas.
- Keep the lawn freshly trimmed.

- Clear away potted plants, as plants indicate work to many people.
- Clear patios or decks of all small items such as small planters, charcoal, barbecues grills, sandboxes, kiddie pools, toys, and more.
- If needed, repaint the house, the trim, the doors (especially the front door), and so on. Choose neutral colors (sage, light gold, pale yellows, or gray).
- Replace the mailbox and the outside light if they're worn, and keep the entryway well lighted. Be sure the house numbers are clearly visible

### Living spaces

- Remove piles of clutter, mail, magazines, catalogs, or books from countertops, desktops, and other surfaces.
- Keep the curtains open so natural light shines in.
- If the room is crowded, remove any unessential furnishings. Dust the remaining furniture.
- Have some fresh flowers visible at each showing. You might even consider paying a local florist to bring a fresh bunch weekly.
- Clean kitchen appliances and the floor after every meal.
- Use a cord bundler to keep nests of wires and cords out of sight.

## What's the easiest way to find a reliable handyman?

Although there are some fantastic companies listed in the yellow pages, it can be time-consuming to make multiple calls. Try www.angieslist.com for local listings and unbiased reviews, including actual client reports. You can also check out www.RentAHusband.com or call 877-99-hubby.

## After a move, how can I unpack in an organized manner?

Although it can be tempting to start ripping through boxes, try to unpack one room at a time in this order:

- Kitchen: Begin here so that you can have snacks to fuel your fire. Items that you don't need right away can be set aside to unpack at a later time when you can better plan the right setup. This is also a good time to line your cabinets and drawers with a shelf liner.
- Bathroom: Get your toiletries out and make sure the toilet, faucets, etc., are operational and clean. A few things you should definitely have on hand first are a shower curtain, toilet paper, and soap.
- Bedrooms: Put major pieces of furniture in place before unpacking. Set up an organized closet next. The person who will claim the bedroom should make the area feel comfortable and personal to them. If you don't have time to set up the bedrooms before the first night, have a family campout instead.
- Living Room: Check out your home's wiring before unpacking the items for this room. The entertainment center will have to be in close proximity to the cable outlet and electrical outlets. Put furniture in place and hook up electronics.
- Garage: Creating an organized garage can be a daunting task. Start by setting up shelves and hooks for placement of tools, yard supplies, etc.

**Note:** Don't forget to collapse boxes for storage or recycling, or you can register them with U-Haul's box exchange.

## I agreed to help my parent downsize thirty years of belongings to move into an assisted living facility. Where should we start?

A project like this is not only overwhelming but can be emotionally draining as well. A good first step is to create a plan. Get the new room measurements. Find out if any furniture or amenities are included and if there are any restrictions from the assisted living facility. Once you know those basics it will be much easier to determine which large items like furniture to bring along or to give away to family or to a charity. Next, block off time on your calendar to work on the project. If you have four months, work backward from the moving deadline to figure our how many days you have to work with. That will determine how fast you have to work.

Setting guidelines early on can go a long way. One guideline may be that any paperwork ten years old or older can be tossed. If it contains sensitive information it goes into a large box marked "shred." That way anyone flipping through paperwork can get down to work instead of asking questions about what needs to be kept. Keep in mind this process is usually emotionally draining; it can be heartbreaking to come upon items that belong to someone no longer with us. Of course, any sentimental family pieces that are due to be passed down to others should be set aside. Give a deadline for picking those items up to the intended recipients. Let them know that if they miss the deadline, the items will go to charity. Label a box for charity and include the charity's phone number. When the box is full, call the charity for a pickup.

## I'd like to organize an emergency kit. What belongs inside?

Knowing you have supplies on hand in an emergency kit can give you peace of mind when a disaster strikes. Make a note on your calendar to rotate the items in the kit every time you change the clocks to daylight saving time. Store your kit in a convenient place known to all family members. Ask your physician or pharmacist about storing prescription medications.

Here are the items the American Red Cross suggests having on hand in an emergency kit:

## *Water*

A minimum three-day supply of water per person, or one gallon per person per day. Remember, water is not just for drinking but for food preparation and sanitation as well.

## *Food*

Store at least a three-day supply of nonperishable food, such as:
Ready-to-eat canned meats, fruits, and vegetables
Canned juices
Salt, sugar, pepper, spices, etc.
Vitamins
Food for infants

## *Tools and supplies*

Mess kits, or paper cups, plates, and plastic utensils
Emergency preparedness manual
Battery-operated radio and extra batteries
Flashlight and extra batteries
Cash or traveler's checks, change
Nonelectric can opener, utility knife
Fire extinguisher: small canister ABC type
Tube tent
Pliers
Tape
Compass
Matches in a waterproof container
Aluminum foil
Plastic storage containers
Signal flare
Paper, pencil
Needles, thread

Medicine dropper
Shut-off wrench, to turn off household gas and water
Whistle
Plastic sheeting
Map of the area (for locating shelters)

## Sanitation
Toilet paper, towelettes
Soap, liquid detergent
Feminine supplies
Personal hygiene items
Plastic garbage bags, ties (for personal sanitation uses)
Plastic bucket with tight lid
Disinfectant
Household chlorine bleach

## Clothing and bedding
At least one complete change of clothing and footwear per person
Sturdy shoes or work boots
Rain gear
Blankets or sleeping bags
Hat and gloves
Thermal underwear
Sunglasses

## Special items
Remember family members with special requirements, such as infants and elderly or disabled persons.

### For baby
Formula

Diapers
Bottles
Powdered milk
Medications

**For adults**
Heart and high blood pressure medication
Insulin
Prescription drugs
Denture needs
Contact lenses and supplies
Extra eyeglasses

**Entertainment (based on the ages of family members)**
Games, playing cards, and books
Portable music device

## What belongs in a basic first-aid kit?

First-aid kits can be purchased ready-made, which can save you time and often money. You'll want one for each car and one for the house. To make your own first-aid kit, include the following.

20 adhesive bandages, various size
1 5 x 9 inch sterile dressing
1 conforming roller gauze bandage
2 triangular bandages
2 3 x 3 inch sterile gauze pads
2 x 4 inch sterile gauze pads
1 roll 3-inch cohesive bandage
2 germicidal hand wipes, or waterless alcohol-based hand sanitizer
6 antiseptic wipes

2 pair large medical grade nonlatex gloves
Adhesive tape, 2-inch width
Antibacterial ointment
Cold pack
Scissors (small, personal)
Tweezers
CPR breathing barrier, such as a face shield
Aspirin or nonaspirin pain reliever
Antidiarrhea medication
Antacid (for stomach upset)
Laxative
Syrup of Ipecac (use to induce vomiting if advised by the Poison
   Control Center)

# Chapter 10

# WORK AND HOME OFFICE

- How can I get prepared and stay motivated to organize my home office?
- Is there a step-by-step plan I can follow for organizing my home office?
- How can I cut down on the number of voice mails I receive each day?
- I travel a lot for work and use the passenger-side car seat as my office. How can I keep that space organized?
- Where's the best place to store the inventory for my home-based business?
- If I work from home, how can I keep my business and personal papers separate?
- How can I remember to take items to and from work?
- I have multiple projects to manage and I'm falling behind. What can I do?
- What should I do with my excess office supplies?
- What can I do to make my desk setup more efficient?
- What's the best way to start my day off on the right foot?
- My "to be filed" pile is out of control. What can I do?
- My files are a mess, but I'm not sure what I'm doing wrong. Is there a system I can use to get them in order?
- How can I better organize my electronic files on my computer?
- Is there anything I can do to save time during my workday?
- How can I have a more productive morning at work?
- What are some suggestions for more organized and efficient meetings?
- How can I remember how to do tasks that usually require an instruction manual?
- How can I actually get to read my "to read" pile?
- Is there a rule for how long to keep professional journals?
- My email inbox is overloaded. What should I do?

## How can I get prepared and stay motivated to organize my home office?

Whether your home office is the dining room table, a desk in the spare bedroom, or an actual home office in a separate room, organizing the space can pose one of your biggest challenges. It's easy to put off filing and accumulate papers that need to be shredded. Beware of the clutter trap; in no time at all, it can build to an overwhelming state. A messy desk and chaotic filing system can waste your time and energy, and cost you money.

Make organizing your home office a one-weekend marathon plan. You won't be able to use the office while you're organizing, so pick a weekend where you can see the jobs through, start to finish. Be forewarned that your office will probably look worse before it looks better, so don't panic. Make organizing fun by playing music. Stay motivated by challenging yourself to beat the clock: set timer and see what you can accomplish in that time. You also can make it a social event by inviting a trusted friend to shred papers and keep you company. Take before and after pictures of the office. The pictures can help in two ways: one, you'll see proof of all your hard work; two, you'll be less likely to let it revert to how it was.

## Is there a step-by-step plan I can follow for organizing my home office?

Yes. Here are eleven steps for getting your home office in order (and keeping it that way) in just one weekend:

### Step 1: Clear the decks
The piles of paper must go. If you have a pile of papers to file, put them all in a single file folder and label it "to file." Don't take the time to file them now. Scoop up other papers, keeping the most

recent on the top of the pile, and put the pile aside. You'll get back to the papers when you have time and space to deal with them.

### Step 2: Make surface space

Take everything off the top of your desk. Clean the desk and then replace only what you use every day: items like your computer, lamp, pens in a cup, and desktop file box.

Photographs and personal mementos are best kept off the desk; a shelf on the wall is a better choice. Keep office equipment like the fax machine and printer within reach but off your desktop.

### Step 3: Dump the drawers

Now is the time to find out what you have in those drawers. Use your newly found surface space to dump out the drawers' contents. Replace only the items you use, storing like items together. Ziplock bags can contain loose pieces easily. Leftover box lids turned upside down work well, too.

### Step 4: Stash the supplies

Avoid keeping excess office supplies in the desk drawers. They cause the drawers to become jam-packed too quickly, and prevent you from finding what you need. Instead, designate one basket or shelf to store supplies. Keep one roll of tape in your desk, and the others in your supply area. That way you can shop at home first.

### Step 5: Don't commingle

Separate home and office if you work from home or have a home-based business. Keep one file drawer for personal paperwork and one for business. You might even need two separate work spaces to keep things really separate. If you don't have two work spaces, try color-coding using two common colors like red and blue (red for personal and blue for business). At a glace, you'll know which bank statements are in the file.

## *Step 6: Shred*

Keep a large trash can, recycling bin, and shredder handy. If you have to search for these items to shred a sensitive document, you're more likely to put it down to do it later. Instead, make it convenient to shred as soon as you come across such documents. Store extra liners nearby, maybe even under the one in the shredder, so you can replace them quickly. Wondering what to shred? The easy answer is anything that has a signature, account number, Social Security number, or medical or legal information (plus credit offers). Here are the specifics:

- Address labels from junk mail and magazines
- ATM receipts
- Bank statements
- Birth certificate copies
- Canceled and voided checks
- Credit and charge card bills, carbon copies, summaries, and receipts
- Credit reports and histories
- Documents containing maiden name (used by credit card companies for security reasons)
- Documents containing names, addresses, phone numbers, or email addresses
- Documents containing passwords or personal identification (PIN) numbers
- Documents relating to investments
- Driver's licenses or items with a driver's license number
- Employee pay stubs
- Employment records

- Expired passports and visas
- Identification cards (college IDs, state IDs, employee ID badges, military IDs)
- Investment, stock, and property transactions
- Items with a signature (leases, contracts, letters)
- Legal documents
- Luggage tags
- Medical and dental records
- Papers with a Social Security number
- Preapproved credit card applications
- Receipts with checking account numbers
- Report cards
- Résumés or curriculum vitae
- Tax forms
- Transcripts
- Travel itineraries
- Used airline tickets
- Utility bills (telephone, gas, electric, water, cable TV, Internet)

### *Step 7: Archival files*

Make sure you have disaster-proof storage bins to tuck away documents you may need to refer to in the future. It's helpful to keep a copy of an important document in disaster-proof storage and another filed. For most families, it is better to store archival documents in bins instead of filing cabinets. A simple two-drawer filing cabinet is a good solution for the current year's papers, but anything beyond that is wasting space. Here's a list of what belongs in your disaster-proof storage bin:

- Automobile insurance cards and policies
- Bank account numbers

- Car registrations and titles
- Cemetery plot deeds
- Certificates of birth or death
- Copy of driver's license
- Deeds
- Homeowner's policy
- Household inventory (try Collectify Home Edition software for the quickest and easiest way to create a home inventory)
- Insurance cards and policies
- Investment records
- Legal papers (such as divorce decrees and property settlement papers)
- Life insurance policy
- Mailing list of family and friends
- Marriage licenses
- Medical history
- Military records
- Papers or records that prove ownership (such as real estate deeds, automobile titles, and stock and bond certificates)
- Personal identification numbers (PINs)
- Photo negatives, one wedding photo, and one baby photo
- Residency letter (a letter from the state sent to you at current address to prove you reside there)
- Social Security cards
- Tax records
- Will/living will or advance directive, or Durable Powers of Attorney for Health Care

These are the items for your more permanent or archived household files:

- Audit reports: Keep forever
- Bank deposit slips: Keep for seven years
- Bank statements: Keep for seven years
- Canceled checks: Keep for seven years
- Current contracts and leases: Keep for life of contract, plus seven years
- Housing records: Keep as long as you own the home, plus seven years (includes home improvements, additions, expenses involved in selling/buying home)
- Insurance records: Keep forever
- Investment records: Keep for seven years after sale of investment (Discard monthly statements once you receive annual summary that reflects yearly activity.)
- IRA contributions: Keep forever
- Legal correspondence: Keep forever (Marriage certificates, death certificates, divorce papers, etc.)
- Real estate records: Keep forever
- Receipts for appliances, computer equipment, etc: Keep for life of asset, plus seven years
- Tax returns and supporting documentation: Keep forever
- Warranties/guarantees: Keep for life of the product

### Step 8: Use wall space

Instead of using only the horizontal space in your office, try looking up. In most offices there is a tremendous amount of wasted vertical space. Look into getting a floor-to-ceiling book-shelf or wall-mounted shelves. Hanging items also allows you to use wasted space. For example, use a wall-mounted CD rack to store CDs, or attach your computer speakers to the wall to free up desk space.

### Step 9: Think outside the file

Make it a habit to file papers in the moment instead of making a pile to be filed. If packed file drawers are making your filing job difficult, then remove a handful of files and weed through them. If your filing cabinet is packed with outdated information, you'll have nowhere to store the current papers.

Keep in mind that traditional file cabinets are not your only option. A multiple-slot accordion file can easily store bill stubs and receipts by month. And a three-ring notebook filled with clear plastic sheet protectors can store appliance manuals.

### Step 10: Piles and files

As you go through your stacks of paper, mountains of magazines, and crates of catalogs, ask yourself: Do I need this? Why? What happens to it next? Where will I look for it when I need it? A filing system won't work if you can't remember where you put things. If you hold on to papers because you aren't sure whether you'll need them again, employ a two-step toss system. Use a large container to collect the papers you think you can part with but aren't totally sure you can. Use a smaller trash can for true garbage items. Empty the large basket only once every few weeks. That way, you can retrieve anything you might change your mind about.

### Step 11: Maintain your new space

Use the two-minute rule to maintain your new space: if you can do a task in two minutes or less, do it at that moment. For example, replace the printer paper, shred the credit card offer, return the email, make the phone call, and file the document. Also, when you finish working in the office each day, take three to five minutes to put everything away.

## How can I cut down on the number of voice mails I receive each day?

Take a moment to record a new outgoing message. In your new message, do the following:

- Give the answers to the top three frequently asked questions, like hours of operation or a fax number.
- Inform callers that they should be calling you for ABC, not XYZ, and suggest they call the appropriate person for XYZ.
- Direct callers to a website for immediate answers.
- Ask callers to describe what they need in a short message. That way, you can find the answer before you call them back, hopefully eliminating an additional call. Plus, if you get their voice mail, you can simply leave the answer.
- Let callers know what time of day you typically return calls and what time you are easiest to reach live by phone.

Adding these five items to your outgoing message will give the caller a better chance of getting the answer he or she needs without even speaking with you live, thus eliminating some of the return calls you need to make.

## I travel a lot for work and use the passenger-side car seat as my office. How can I keep that space organized?

Use a mobile office organizer. Find a bin at home to make your own or purchase one at a local office supply store. Sit this container on the passenger seat within reach so you have a place for all your necessities. Then, when you have a passenger, you have only one thing to move out of the way. You might find it helpful to further contain smaller items like makeup in ziplock bags so you don't lose them. Clear bags allow you to easily find what you need. For coupons, receipts, and the like, try a sun visor CD holder. Its slots are perfect for holding coupons and receipts for the month.

## Where's the best place to store the inventory for my home-based business?

This will depend on the size and quantity of what you have to store safely. Flooring samples or scrapbooking supplies take up much more space than makeup, but makeup needs to be stored away from extreme heat or cold. Before deciding on where to store the inventory, consider:

- Temperature and light requirements
- Ease of reach
- Quantity
- Ease of transporting
- Possible future increase
- Weight

Once you're clear on the above points, then you can choose the location for storage. Possibilities include shelving in a garage or a shelving unit or bookcase in the basement. You can also give up a closet to store supplies, or add a closet organizer or shelving to a closet that's in use. Another option is to add an armoire in a room or hallway.

## If I work from home, how can I keep my business and personal papers separate?

If possible, give yourself two separate and distinct workspaces. Two desks would be ideal, but most rooms won't allow for that. The alternative is a single desk and two file drawers: one for business and one for personal. Use color-coding to designate a specific color file folder for work files and another for personal files. Two small rolling file carts might be a good solution; that way, you can pull up the one you need depending on what you are working on. Be sure to put away projects when you are finished working on them—don't leave out business papers when you start to pay personal bills, for example.

## How can I remember to take items to and from work?

Designate a single tote bag in an eye-catching color, like red or yellow, for transporting items to and from work. Hang the tote on the office and home front doorknobs so you'll remember to carry it with you. When you place something in it at one location, always empty it at the other location. Otherwise, you'll end up with a jam-packed tote bag. It may take a week or two to get into your new routine, but once you do you'll always know where to place the item you want to take with you—and where to find the item you brought with you. The tote bag is also the perfect place to clip a reminder note to yourself, since the tote is the last thing you'll touch on the way out the door.

## I have multiple projects to manage and I'm falling behind. What can I do?

Use your calendar to help organize your projects. Note the due date for the first project on the calendar. On the day before the due date, jot down a reminder that it is due the next day. Then work backward, blocking off enough time on the calendar to work on the project in order to meet the deadline. Include buffer time, as you never know what might send your project into a tailspin. Be sure your goals are realistic and check what else you already have going on. It would be unrealistic to think you could wrap up a project on a day when you're going to be at a meeting most of the day, so plan accordingly. Finally, make notes about anything you might need to buy in order to complete the project on time. For example, if you need to print something out, you don't want to find out you're out of printer paper at the last minute.

## What should I do with my excess office supplies?

No one needs six rolls of tape in the desk drawer, so store all the excess items away from the items you use every day. Also, store like items together. For example, place all the writing instruments in one clearly labeled container and all printer ink cartridges in another. Leave a pack of sticky notes nearby so when you use up an item you can write yourself a quick reorder reminder. Also keep a master list nearby with model numbers, where to buy the item, or any other special information. That way, you won't have to dig out the instruction manual each time you need to reorder something like printer cartridges.

## What can I do to make my desk setup more efficient?

The best thing to do is to keep what you need within reach: pens in a pen cup on top of the desk, a stapler in the top desk drawer, a calculator nearby, and so on. If these basic items aren't handy, you'll waste valuable time looking for them. Next, organize the desk drawers. The front part of the top drawer is easiest to access, so use it to store the items you use most often. Use the front of the second drawer for items used frequently but not as often as those in the first drawer. Save the backs of the drawers for less commonly used office items. Use drawer dividers to keep things in their place as you open and close the drawers. Tuck personal items like photos of loved ones on a nearby shelf or wall to keep them off of your workspace.

## What's the best way to start my day off on the right foot?

You might be surprised to learn that the best way to ensure a smooth start to your day is by wrapping up the prior day. As each day comes to a close, spend five or ten minutes filing papers, tidying up your desk, checking your calendar, making your to-do list for the next day, and pulling out any files you'll need. Then you can start the next day with a clean slate, ready to hit the ground running instead of wrapping up yesterday's loose ends.

## My "to be filed" pile is out of control. What can I do?

Some people suggest scheduling a time to do your filing, and for some that advice might work. However, most people would probably skip the filing even if they'd scheduled it on their calendar. The best way to deal with the pile of filing is to not make one in the first place. It's possible if you change your habit. Chances are you're not filing the papers immediately because (1) there's no system in place so you don't know what to do with the papers; (2) the place you file papers is inconvenient, and it's easier to just put them down to deal with them later; or (3) the filing system is so clogged with papers that there's no more room to file the papers. If you don't have a working system, set one up quickly using the directions on pages 192–195. If you already have a system in place but the filing cabinet is difficult to access, try moving it closer to you. Imagine printing a document that you need to file and simply turning your chair to the right, pulling open a drawer, and filing it immediately. It would be so easy, you couldn't help but file. If you can't bring over the entire filing cabinet, then opt for something smaller like a single filing basket or a rolling file cart. Then, when it gets full, you can bring it to the filing cabinet. If the filing system is overflowing with paper and you can't fit in even one more document, however, you have to purge the files. Either set aside short blocks of time to go through a handful of files at a time, or grab a file box, toss in a good number of outdated files, label the box, and store it away. You'll still have the files should you need to access them, and you'll have plenty of room to file new papers.

## My files are a mess, but I'm not sure what I'm doing wrong. Is there a system I can use to get them in order?

Yes, follow these pointers and action steps to set up a system that works for you.

### System key 1: Separate current files from archival files

There are two basic types of files: temporary (working) files, which are the ones you reference once a month or more, and permanent (archival) files, which are the ones you refer to less than once a month, like tax returns.

### System key 2: Label all files

Each file must have a title. Shy away from broad titles such as Urgent, My Stuff, and To Do. Instead, make a label that reflects what's inside the file, like Home Decorating Ideas, or Prospects to Call.

### System key 3: Store the files

When deciding how and where to store the files, run through this checklist:

- Who will use the files, when and where?
- Do you need to reach the files while sitting at a desk?
- Is security an issue requiring the files to be locked? Most likely the files will go in several areas. For example, you might be

working on a file and store it in a wall file system near your desk, then put it into a nearby file drawer until the project is complete, then recycle it or store it away.

### System key 4: Create a filing system

Create a filing system that makes sense to you and that you use consistently. Here are some of the most popular choices:

- Alphabetical by topic (filing under U for utilities or P for phone is better than filing under V for Verizon or C for Comcast Cable)
- Subject—for example, designate a hanging file for Bills and place manila folders inside for each type of recurring bill.
- Numerical—excellent for dated material, such as purchase orders.
- Tickler file with thirty-one files or slots labeled one through thirty-one to represent the days of the month. Slide the paper in the correct dated file and check the file daily so you always have what you need on the day you need it. This system is perfect for very detailed tasks such as tracking bills and correspondence.

### Action step 1

Make sure your shredder is in working order, plug it in, and keep it nearby.

### Action step 2

Set aside eighteen minutes of time to weed through a handful of files in the filing cabinet, purging files as necessary.

### Action step 3

Work for another eighteen minutes or until you have at least half a drawer of space.

### Action step 4
Gather your filing supplies, labels, folders (manila and hanging), tabs, label maker, and sticky notes.

### Action step 5
Set your timer for eighteen minutes. Pick up the top paper from the closest paper pile and take action: save it, shred it, recycle it, read it. Make a decision and follow through.

### Action step 6
Go through the papers in small blocks of time, asking questions like: When was that last time I needed this? Am I going to read this before it's out of date? Can I get this again if I need it? Am I the only one with a copy? What's the worst thing that can happen if I toss this?

### Action step 7
If you're stuck about whether to save something, try a two-step toss. Designate one box as the two-step toss box. If you're really unsure about the item, toss it in the box and save it for a month or two. If you need it, then it's there; if you don't use it within that time period, recycle it.

### Action step 8
Take action on every new piece of paper that comes your way. Don't just put it down—put it away.

### Be prepared
Make it as easy as possible to add new files to your system. Keep a stock of labels, folders (manila and hanging), tabs, and other filing materials handy. Be ready to quickly create a home for any lost piece of paper. It takes less than two minutes to create a new file, so take

control of the papers and stop piling them up. A great filing system is the key to calming the chaos.

## How can I better organize my electronic files on my computer?

Within the software programs you use most often, name your files and folders with names that match the paper version of your files. For example, if you have text files and paper files for ongoing projects, name the hanging file folder and the computer folder with the name of the category. This will simplify both systems and lessen the chance of you forgetting where things are located. Also stop saving files to your desktop. It's difficult to find the file you need in a mess of icons.

## Is there anything I can do to save time during my workday?

Yes, here are three things you can do to save time during the workday:

1. Write notes in the right place the first time. Instead of jotting notes on any scrap of paper that is handy at the moment, take an extra second and find the correct place to write it down the first time. This will eliminate time-consuming rewriting. For example, if someone is giving you his or her new cell phone number, grab your address book and write it there instead of writing it on a piece of paper and having to transfer it later.

2. Move extra seating away from your desk. If there is a chair nearby, push it to the far corner. An empty chair is an invitation to someone walking by to stop in, sit down, and have a chat, even if you are short on time. Plus, empty chairs usually don't stay empty very long; they tend to be a drop zone for all sorts

of stuff to "get to later." In the meantime, you might waste time looking for stuff you need that's lost in the pile.

3. Confirm appointments ahead of time. Taking an extra moment to call and confirm that an appointment is still on and running on time can save you precious time. You cannot depend on the other person to notify you if they're running late or if an appointment has been cancelled. By taking that extra time to confirm appointments, you avoid wasting time traveling to an appointment only to find out it has been cancelled, or arriving on time for an appointment and having to wait when you could have been using your time more constructively.

## How can I have a more productive morning at work?

Don't check your voice mail and email at the start of each workday. As you check voice mail and email, you're off and running, and the day can get away from you. You might return a call right away, or start finding the answer you need to return the call. Once you open email messages, it's easy to start clicking links and going online. Before you know, hours can elapse, and you'll be no closer to accomplishing the items on your to-do list. If you set aside some quiet time in the morning before you dive in to your messages, you can use those fifteen, twenty, or even thirty minutes to work on a piece of a larger project to keep it moving along.

## What are some suggestions for more organized and efficient meetings?

Here are my top ten suggestions for meetings that work:

1. If the meeting will be brief, conduct it standing up. It will be less formal and go faster.

2. Only invite the necessary people to attend. The fewer the people, the faster the meeting goes.
3. Prior to the meeting, pass out written agendas with a time frame for each topic to be discussed. Place the start time and end time on the agenda. Note in bold if someone is responsible for bringing something to the meeting.
4. At the start of the meeting, request that everyone turn off their cell phones and turn pagers to vibrate.
5. Designate someone as the timekeeper; this person will also be responsible for keeping the meeting on track. Rotate this duty from meeting to meeting.
6. Have everyone stand and stretch every thirty minutes. Attention spans are only about that long.
7. Add a question-and-answer period at the end of the meeting. Let people know it is coming so they can save their questions until then. Most likely, their questions will be answered during the meeting.
8. Should someone have a very specific question, ask to speak with them one-on-one after the meeting.
9. At the end of the meeting, recap what was discussed and who is responsible for what so that everyone is on the same page.
10. Make someone responsible for taking notes and distributing them within forty-eight hours of the meeting. Make sure action items are noted in bold.

## How can I remember how to do tasks that usually require an instruction manual?

Create "cheat sheets" or mini reminders for tasks that you don't do routinely, and keep them near where you'll need them. Instead of having to refer to a manual or wasting time trying to figure out a task, you can look at your notes and quickly find exactly what to do.

## How can I actually get to read my "to read" pile?

Before you toss another paper on top of the already towering pile, ask yourself two questions: Can I skim this now instead of putting it off? Do I really intend on reading this? You might just have a bad habit of putting paper on the pile. If you stop and think first, you can just read the item quickly or decide that you don't need to read it at all. If you opt to skim the document and learn that it requires more in-depth reading, at least you've already started it and you can add it to the pile. Instead of a single towering "to read" pile try two piles—one pile for what you truly intend to read, the other for what you most likely won't read. Make a note on your calendar whenever you expect to have a few minutes of free time to read, like when you have a doctor's appointment, when you're picking someone up from the airport, or even when you're picking up your children from school. Grab something small from the top of the first "to read" pile and carry it with you, to finally read. If you get through the first "to read" pile, you can start reading the second pile of papers.

## Is there a rule for how long to keep professional journals?

The rule of thumb is keep journals for the current year only. Going past the current year generally means you're keeping outdated information. Remember that you can usually order a back issue directly from the publisher in the event you ever need one. Often, journal articles are available online at no charge for print subscribers. You might consider sharing a single subscription with someone else in your profession. Also, check with your local library; sometimes libraries are willing to take in back issues for circulation. By taking back issues to the library, you can still get to them if you need them, you are sharing them, and—best of all—you don't have to store them.

## My email inbox is overloaded. What should I do?

Most of us are great at reading email messages. Acting on them or deleting them is another story. Try working in short intervals of time. Read and act on each email. You have four basic choices:

1. Keep (in a folder not your inbox)
2. Delete
3. Flag as spam
4. Reply/act

Try not print the emails. That just makes for more paper clutter. If you need to save an email, put it in a folder or copy and paste it into a Word document you can then save. Here are some helpful tips no matter which email service you use:

- Reply to anyone who sends you broadcast emails like the joke of the day and ask him or her to remove your email address until you can get your inbox under control.
- Whenever you can, use the phone rather than sending an email.
- When you write emails, use a descriptive subject line that relates to something in the message so you can find the one you need easily.
- Try opening a second email account that you don't plan on checking often. Use it for the purpose of registrations on websites or for order confirmations. Reserve your personal email account for friends and family.
- Save a copy of important emails in your sent box so if the recipient does not receive the email, you can resend it instead of rewriting it.

Depending on which email service you use, you might be able to take advantage of these tips. Use the ones you can; they all help.

- Color-code your incoming emails. Choose three colors and assign them to specific senders, so when you see that color you'll automatically know who sent the message.
- Set up folders in your inbox as a place to save emails instead of keeping them all in your inbox.
- Sort the emails by sender so all of the emails from a specific sender will be grouped together.
- The best tip is to consistently set aside time (daily or weekly) to deal with email. Set aside time not just to read emails but to act on them. You don't need a lot of time; you just need to make time consistently.

- What's the best way to stay focused?
- How can I stop waking up at night thinking of everything I need to do?
- How can I get tasks done more quickly?
- How can I stop procrastinating?
- I have trouble keeping up with the laundry. Can you suggest a routine for getting it done?
- How can I keep matching socks together?
- Is it possible for someone to multitask and be successful?
- My plans always seem to fall apart. Is there any way I can avoid this?
- How does preparing the night before ease the morning rush?
- I find myself wasting time waiting for appointments to start. My hairdresser and even the veterinarian always seem to be running late. What can I do?
- How can I spend less time running errands?
- I do silly things like not changing my car's windshield wiper blades when needed. Then when it rains I have to drive slower because I can't see well, or I have to stop at the shop to get new ones. I feel like I make my own difficulties. What can I do?
- How can I gracefully end phone calls with chatty acquaintances?
- How can I break the bad habit of watching TV shows just because they're on?
- What is the most effective time management technique?
- How can I overcome feeling guilty when I say no to volunteering my time?
- I find myself playing endless games of phone tag with people I need to reach. What can I do?
- How can I remember what days my favorite restaurants are closed or the hours of operation for the local home goods store?
- How can I be better prepared for special events?
- How can I get out the door with what I need?
- How can I make better use of my time each day?
- How can I take care of home repairs before they become overwhelming?
- How can I stop running from room to room to grab things I need?
- How can I keep items for a project conveniently in one place?
- How can I stop forgetting things?

- How can I stay motivated to be organized?
- How can I remember to check my calendar?
- Is there a way to stop transcribing information onto my calendar from other sources?
- How can I leave the house without forgetting necessary items like my car keys and cell phone?
- What's one tip for saving time starting tomorrow?
- What are the biggest time wasters?
- I do everything; how can I get others to pitch in?
- Is there a most productive time of day?
- Can wearing an apron save me time and keep me more organized?

## What's the best way to stay focused?

Use "cake-baking focus." Once you put a cake in the oven, in order not to burn it you have to stay focused. You might set a timer, or at least stay near the oven to keep a close watch. That's the kind of focus you need to stay organized. When you're working on a task, act as if you were baking a cake. Set a timer to keep you on target, and stay there. Don't get sidetracked until you've accomplished the task at hand. Often the task at hand is just a portion of a bigger task. Use cake-baking focus for small, incremental tasks until the larger task is completed.

## How can I stop waking up at night thinking of everything I need to do?

At least an hour before bedtime each night, make a list of things to do. If you wait until too close to bedtime, you won't have time to process the ideas and they'll keep you up. This list does not have to be in any particular order, and you don't have to spell things correctly or even write legibly. The idea is to simply get the list out of your head and onto paper. Most likely you'll pick one or two items from the list to add to your to-do list. The other stuff can stay on the list, and not in your head.

## How can I get tasks done more quickly?

Use the "egg timer rule." This rule says that if you can do a task in three minutes or less, you should do it right then. Cooks usually set an egg timer for three minutes when cooking a soft-boiled egg. In three minutes or less there, you can wrap up plenty of tasks. For example, you could hang a jacket on a peg upon entering the house instead of hanging it on the back of a chair; you could sort the pile of mail over the recycling bin instead of leaving it on the kitchen counter; or you could RSVP to a party invitation that you just received. When you take care of the task at hand instead of leaving it for later, you feel more accomplished.

## How can I stop procrastinating?

Often, people spend more time thinking about completing a task than actually completing it. There are several ways to stop putting things off. Go public—tell others what you're doing so they can help to hold you accountable. Since you won't want to disappoint them, you'll be more likely to follow through. Finding support is another good way to get things accomplished. Try asking someone to help you or at least keep you company as you work. Talking through a task with someone can provide the support you need to get it done. Many times, tasks without deadlines can be left to linger.

Setting your own deadline gives you a goal to reach. For example, if you want to clear out your wardrobe closet, schedule an appointment with a closet organization company for a free estimate. The appointment will act as your motivator. Other times, consider whether you're the best person to do the job. Delegating the job to someone else is sometimes a good solution for undone tasks. Rewarding yourself for a job well done, or at least a good start to the job, can sometimes be all the incentive you need to act. Scheduling a manicure for late in the day after you've organized the kitchen pantry can help you avoid procrastinating. Finally, try breaking up the task into smaller, more manageable steps. Often, people procrastinate because tasks are overwhelming or they're not sure what to do. For example, if "write holiday cards" is on your to-do list, chances are you won't do it. The task is too abstract. But if you list manageable tasks like "determine number of holiday cards to buy" or "update address book, then print labels for cards," you're more likely to act on them.

## I have trouble keeping up with the laundry. Can you suggest a routine for getting it done?

You're not the only one who feels like you're always doing the laundry. Here's a simple routine for taking control:

1.  Decide where you want dirty clothing to gather. You might decide on one clothes hamper per bedroom, or one hamper per bathroom. Or maybe you want all the laundry brought to the laundry room. If that's the case, a triple laundry sorter in the laundry area makes it easy to stay organized. The triple sorter allows each person to sort his own laundry as he drops it off, saving you from having to do the sorting.

2.  Institute a new family rule that all dirty clothing goes in the right place every day. Clarify what constitutes dirty; for example, a shirt worn for ten minutes might not be dirty. Make a rule about how clothes need to be placed in the hamper (jean legs not rolled, pockets empty, etc.). If dirty clothes aren't left in the designated space, hold the clothes for ransom: simply hold on to an article of clothing until its owner completes an extra chore. Tell family members that you'll keep anything you find in the pockets of dirty clothes. Use a magnet to attach a plastic ziplock bag to the washer to

collect loose items. Label laundry bins so family members can sort darks, lights, and whites for you. Or, use a triple sorter so you can skip the step of sorting and just wash.

3. Check your calendar and designate two days each week for laundry. Note them on the calendar and notify everyone that these are the designated laundry days.

4. Twice a week collect, wash, dry, and fold the laundry. Decide whether you will return the clean clothing to family members' bedrooms, whether you want them to pick up their clothing from the laundry room, or whether you will put away the clothes in dressers and closets.

5. As you do the laundry, set aside items that need mending and items that you want to donate to charity. Placing a bag in your closet for charity is a great way to start collecting items.

6. Create a checklist of all the items you like to have on hand for the laundry task: detergents, dryer sheets, fabric softener, bleach, stain remover, and so on. Check your list weekly and replace items that are running low.

7. If you have items that require dry cleaning, consider using a service that offers pickup and delivery. If that's not possible, pick a day for dry cleaning and note it on the calendar. If you have a tangle of dry cleaning hangers that need a home, purchase a hanger holder to contain them.

8. At the start of every month, check the family calendar to see what special clothing needs you may have. For example, for Earth Day at school, your child might need a green T-shirt. For a black-tie affair, you might need your little black dress. Plan ahead so such items are clean for the events.

9. Add mending to your calendar and do it every month. There probably will only be a few pieces each month, and it may not seem worth it to schedule the task. However, it's

quicker to replace two buttons than waiting until more need
to be replaced.

## How can I keep matching socks together?

Use a lingerie bag—the mesh pull-string type meant for delicates—
for each family member's socks. The bag will keep socks together in
the wash. Stray socks often fall over the edge of the washer drum
and can ruin the washer. More socks are lost in the washer than in
the dryer. Another option for keeping socks matched throughout
the laundering process is a clothespin for each pair. With a little
organization on the front end, you won't have to match piles of
clean socks.

## Is it possible for someone to multitask and be successful?

My opinion is that no one can multitask successfully. When you
divide your attention, things take longer, you make mistakes, and
your forget things. It is possible to double up, choosing a mindless
task like shredding papers (that have already been sorted) while
watching a movie, or helping a child with homework while cooking
dinner. But when two tasks both require attention to detail, brainpower, and focus, they can't be completed at the same time—at
least not successfully.

## My plans always seem to fall apart. Is there any way I can avoid this?

Instead of making plans, set goals. A plan is a rigid pass-or-fail
benchmark, such as leaving the house by 8:00 a.m. Either you leave
by that time or you don't. Most times you don't, so you've failed
already. Instead, try setting a goal of leaving between 7:45 and 8:00
a.m. More likely than not, you'll be out the door consistently by

8:00 and feel good about yourself. Look at your plans closely; they might include goals that are impossible to reach. Keep your goals flexible and realistic.

## How does preparing the night before ease the morning rush?

Most households experience a morning rush, time when many tasks need to be completed in a specific amount of time. Some people are not at their best in the morning, making these tasks even more challenging. However, with a little organization the night before, you can avoid racing around in the morning trying to pick out an outfit, find your keys, and whatever else you need to start your day. To ensure a calm morning, spend several minutes the night before, to pick out your outfit for the next day, iron it if needed, or sew on any buttons that may have come loose. Pick your accessories and watch. Find your keys, purse, briefcase, and anything else you will need for the day. You can even set the table for breakfast.

Make a to-do list of five to seven things you need to take care of the next day and make sure you have all the necessary information to do them, for example, phone numbers if you need to make calls. Then, you can start your day calm and relaxed, instead of in a mad rush.

## I find myself wasting time waiting for appointments to start. My hairdresser and even the veterinarian always seem to be running late. What can I do?

When making an appointment, try to get the first one of the day or the first one after lunch. There's a better chance you'll be taken on time. Sometimes, though, delayed appointments are inevitable. Always bring something from the top of your to-read pile, so you can catch up on organizing while you're in the waiting room.

## How can I spend less time running errands?

Run all your errands at one time. Start with the one farthest away from your house and finish up with the one closest to your house. Make a list before you go and gather all the things you need in one spot to ensure you have them with you while you're out. If you need to pick up something that needs to be kept cold, toss a cool pack in your car to keep it cold while you drive.

## I do silly things like not changing my car's windshield wiper blades when needed. Then when it rains I have to drive slower because I can't see well, or I have to stop at the shop to get new ones. I feel like I make my own difficulties. What can I do?

Remember that emergencies cost more than planned maintenance. Take in your car for regular servicing and make regular doctor appointments for yourself and your family. Take your pets to the veterinarian regularly, and take care of minor home repairs before they become big ones. Many unexpected and often costly emergencies could have been prevented. Take all the precautions you can to save your time, money, and sanity.

## How can I gracefully end phone calls with chatty acquaintances?

When you need to call someone who you know can be chatty, start the call by saying "I only have a minute, but I wanted to call to…." If the person calls you, start the conversation by saying something like, "I'm glad you caught me, I've only got a minute." Hopefully, by setting the stage you can keep the length of the call to a bare minimum. You can also ask the person whether he or she has a lot to cover, or if he or she could please send you an email instead. If all else fails, wrap up the call by saying something like, "I don't mean to be rude, but I have to cut you off. I really do have to go."

## How can I break the bad habit of watching TV shows just because they're on?

Record the programs you do like, then watch them later. This will save you time two ways: (1) you can skip the commercials, and (2) you can watch your show and turn off the television; another show will not automatically start. If you turn off the TV for just one extra hour a week, you'll save an extra fifty-two hours a year. If you don't own a recording device or are simply technology-challenged not to worry, watch the show live, but do a little task at each commercial break. A one-hour show has about twenty-two minutes of commercial time. That's plenty of time to reorganize a junk drawer, sort the mail, or put away a load of laundry.

## What is the most effective time management technique?

The most effective time management tool is learning to say no, gracefully of course. Before you say yes to anything, ask yourself what you'll be saying no to. There's a tradeoff; every time you agree to one thing, you have less time, or no time, for something else. After all, there are only twenty-four hours in the day. Mastering the art of saying no gracefully is not an easy thing to do; it takes practice. A great way to start practicing is to put a policy in place. Come up with a phrase and practice saying it out loud until it rolls off your tongue Yours might be, "I'm sorry I only do two volunteer projects a year and I've already got mine for this year," or "I have to check with my family." You also can offer an alternative. For example, if you're asked to help with the bake sale for an organization you belong to, offer to make a monetary donation or provide other assistance instead of staying up all night baking.

## How can I overcome feeling guilty when I say no to volunteering my time?

Realize that every time you say yes to someone else, you're also saying no to yourself. There is only so much one person can do and do well. There are a few insider tricks to learning to say no gracefully and without guilt. Come up with a line that you feel comfortable saying, such as any of the following: "I'm sorry, my plate is too full right now; I know I wouldn't do a good job." "I'm sorry; that's our family night. Thank you for thinking of me, but I can't. Let me check my calendar and get back to you." "Unfortunately, I can't; I hope you can find someone else." "I'd love to, but I'm busy that day/night." "I've got something personal to attend to that day." "Normally I'd say yes, but I'm just overbooked right now." Then practice that phrase so that it rolls off your tongue the next time you are approached. Consider choosing your volunteer activities before they choose you. If you're computer proficient, you might volunteer to be in charge of your club's newsletter, so that you can work at home and at convenient times. Once you've accepted a responsibility it will be easier to decline other requests for your time.

## I find myself playing endless games of phone tag with people I need to reach. What can I do?

Try returning phone calls right before lunch or at the end of the day. There's a better chance that you'll catch the person and that he or she won't be very chatty when you do talk. If you still get voice mail, try leaving a message that includes two options for times to reach you. You also can leave a message detailing exactly why you're calling and asking them to leave you a message with the answer. Offering your email address is another option; some people are better with email than with voice mail. Or, you can ask to schedule a time to talk to make things simple for both of you.

## How can I remember what days my favorite restaurants are closed or the hours of operation for the local home goods store?

Keep the hours of operation for the places you frequent in a handy place like the sun visor of your car. This will save you from wasting a ton of time by driving to a store only to find that it's closed. If you prefer a more high-tech solution, enter the info into your cell phone. Start all restaurant entries with the letter 'R'; that way they will all be grouped together and easy to locate. You can also enter hours of operation and even favorite menu items.

## How can I be better prepared for special events?

Check your calendar at the beginning of each month to see what's coming up. That way you can prepare ahead of time. If you need special clothing or gifts for the event, add those tasks to your to-do list. Ensure your success by writing on the calendar where you are placing the items. For example, "birthday party gift in front hall closet."

## How can I get out the door with what I need?

Hang a tote bag on the handle of the door you use most often or on a hook near the leaving station. In the tote place the items you need to take with you: bills to mail, videos or library books to return, driving directions, play tickets, and so on. As you leave, grab the tote, and you'll have everything you need. Make this new plan successful by always bringing the tote back into the house and hanging it up so it can be filled for the next day.

## How can I make better use of my time each day?

Take work or a small handful of reading material with you when you know there's a good chance you'll have a wait. While you're in the car waiting to pick up a child from sports practice or waiting for an appointment or meeting, you can balance your checkbook, write thank-you notes, read a magazine, or even return phone calls. To ensure you have what you need to do the task, pack your tote bag in advance. Also pack a clipboard so you have a hard writing surface. To take advantage of gaps of time while you're at home, keep an informal running list on the inside of your kitchen cabinet for tasks like checking that the pens in the pen cup work or shredding the "to be shred" pile.

## How can I take care of home repairs before they become overwhelming?

Many tasks and chores are associated with maintaining a home, from replacing a lightbulb to fixing a squeaky door. Individually, they take just a small amount of time. But when a few tasks pile up, it takes a lot of time to complete them. Try planning one night or weekend day each month to deal with these tasks. By designating a specific time for them, you can complete a few tasks at the same time. Plus, it won't seem like you're constantly doing a repair or reminding a partner about a repair.

## How can I stop running from room to room to grab things I need?

Store items where you need them. This may mean duplicating some things, like keeping a handheld vacuum, cleaning supplies, scissors, and a telephone in each room where they might be needed. Imagine the time you'll save when you can answer the phone without having to run into a different room or down a flight of stairs to locate it. This rule can be applied outside the home, too. For example, keep a pair of sunglasses in each car, or one in your purse and one in your tote bag.

## How can I keep items for a project conveniently in one place?

Create caddies for recurring projects. Options include a bill-paying caddy that has stamps and return address labels, a cleaning caddy with multipurpose cleaner and rags, and a sandwich caddy that has all the items needed to make a sandwich so you do not have to search the refrigerator.

## How can I stop forgetting things?

Usually we forget things because we are not paying close attention. Stop and think things through as you do them, and chances are your memory will improve instantly. For example, as you place your keys on the hook by the door, say to yourself, *my keys are hanging on the hook by the front door.* Also try these seven techniques to help you remember other important information:

1. Write it down in a single place, like a spiral notebook just for this purpose, where you'll look later on.
2. Use sticky notes (e.g., a note on bathroom mirror).
3. Keep it together (e.g., in a spiral notebook).
4. Call your own phone number and leave yourself a voice mail message.
5. Record yourself on a mini–tape recorder.
6. Email yourself.
7. Set a timer or alarm.

## How can I stay motivated to be organized?

There are a few key ways to maintain your motivation. Chances are you'll need to alternate the ways in which you stay motivated since always resorting to the same solution will likely become monotonous. Here are some tips:

- Before and after pictures: Sometimes simply seeing how it was or your dream of how you want it to be can be enough to get you moving.
- Support: Once you start to look for it, you might be surprised where you'll find support. It might be in the form of a book club, or an online community or message board.
- Go public: Simply tell others about your goal. This is one of the most effective ways to stay motivated.
- Declutter buddy: Teaming up with someone who is generally organized or who is looking to get more organized can be just the motivator you need.
- Even pace: Instead of going full speed ahead and then burning out, try to pace yourself. It can be tempting to overdo it when you find yourself on a roll, but if you do you'll soon find yourself too tired to continue and not too anxious to get back to the project.
- Rewards: Reward yourself as you hit milestones in the project time line. Instead of dreaming up extravagant rewards or rewarding yourself with a shopping trip, simply hold off on something you enjoy until after you've met your goal. If you enjoy a particular blended drink from a local café, don't buy one until your task is complete.

## How can I remember to check my calendar?

If you jot things on your calendar only to forget to check it, thus defeating the purpose of calendar reminders, you're not alone. Avoid this frustration by leaving the calendar in plain sight, for example, on a kitchen wall by the phone or on one corner of the kitchen counter. For a few weeks, leave yourself a reminder note to check the calendar. You can place a sticky note on the bathroom mirror or your coffee mug. After a few weeks of consistently checking the calendar, it will become a habit.

## Is there a way to stop transcribing information onto my calendar from other sources?

Probably not. Spending a moment or two transcribing information from a flyer or schedule onto your calendar is inevitable. Writing in the school cafeteria menu, soccer practices, the scouting schedule, and other important dates on the calendar makes sense. In the long run, you save time by not having to check two places for information and knowing that you don't run the risk of double-booking yourself.

## How can I leave the house without forgetting necessary items like my car keys and cell phone?

Wherever possible, run items out to your car as you think of them, so they'll already be there when you leave. This is especially helpful because you'll have less to carry on your way out later. Placing a sticky note reminder by the doorknob of the door you leave through can also work. Keep the necessary items close to the door so you can simply grab them on your way out. I call this a leaving station. Place an over-the-door clear plastic shoe holder on the wall or on the back of a door nearest the door you use most often. The clear pockets are a perfect fit for all of life's accessories such as keys, cell phone with power cord, sunglasses, bills to be mailed, and movies or books to return.

## What's one tip for saving time starting tomorrow?

Prepare in the evening. By doing all you can before you go to sleep, you ensure a much smoother start to your day. There are many tasks you can complete the night before, like setting the table for breakfast, choosing your outfit to wear the next day, checking the calendar, checking the weather report to see if you need an umbrella, gassing up your car, finding your keys, gathering accessories, placing your purse by the front door, putting coffee in the coffeemaker, and making your lunch, to name just a few.

## What are the biggest time wasters?

There are many time wasters, but these are the biggest ones:

- Television: watching a show you do not absolutely love just because it is on
- Internet surfing: reading "junk" emails and signing up for giveaways
- "Gooey" people: spending time with people who stick to you and weigh you down, instead of the people who are joyful to be around and make you feel good
- Gossiping: participating in senseless chatter about others
- Working on a project without a plan: taking longer to complete a project and making time-consuming mistakes
- Starting a project without all the pieces you need: for example, printing photos without an extra ink cartridge on hand; if you run out, you have to trek to the store
- Not storing items where you use them: running all over the house looking for things that are better stored right where you need them
- Looking for misplaced items: including searching for scrap pieces of paper with important names and numbers on it, now buried in a pile of mail.
- Doing things for people who should be doing them for themselves: picking up your spouse's socks, your daughter's coat, and your son's card collection, which zaps your energy to do other tasks
- Allowing yourself to become distracted and/or sidetracked

## I do everything; how can I get others to pitch in?

First, determine if you might be contributing to the problem. Do you shoo away others who try to help, or redo their work (like refolding towels) that isn't up to your standards? If that's the case, then try saying yes when others offer to help. Even if you don't feel you really need the help, it can be a great way to let others pitch in. Delegate the work and let the results stand; after all, there's more than one way to fold towels. It is actually selfish for you to do everything, because you're not allowing others to learn and grow. If a child never learns how to pack a backpack at a young age, he or she won't know how to do it later on.

## Is there a most productive time of day?

Yes, each person has a time of day when she is most sharp and able to concentrate on detail-oriented projects. Some people are "early risers," and others are "night owls." Get to know your prime time and use it to your advantage. The best projects to do during prime time are those that require patience and concentration, like balancing your checking account.

## Can wearing an apron save me time and keep me more organized?

Yes, but only if the apron has pockets. Wearing an apron with pockets lets you keep items you need close at hand. The obvious use is to wear one while cooking, but try wearing an apron while cleaning to hold cleaning supplies. Or wear one while packing boxes; use the pockets to keep tape and scissors within reach. Gift wrapping and gardening are two other activities that can be made easier when you wear an apron to hold tools and keep clothes clean.

# Chapter 12

# SIMPLY GREEN ORGANIZING

- What common household items can I repurpose for organizing?
- My bookshelf is out of room. What should I do?
- How can I avoid buying wrapping paper?
- What can I do with furniture I'd like to use in nontraditional ways?
- Cases of bottled water take up lots of space in my pantry. Once used, the bottles fill up my recycling bin. Is there a way to organize this clutter?
- I'd like to organize a recycling center at home. How do I get started?
- Is there a better way to organize the tangle of wire hangers from the dry cleaner?
- How can I remember to take canvas bags to the store?
- How can I organize all of my household cleaners?
- How can I use or reuse dryer sheets for organizing and cleaning up?
- What's the best way to recycle items such as cell phones and batteries?

## What common household items can I repurpose for organizing?

There are hundreds of items already in your home that you can repurpose. However, it takes some practice to look past an item's original purpose and see a new way of using it. Eventually, it won't take long for you to come up with new and creative ways to use items instead of tossing them in the garbage. Here are a few thoughts to get you started:

- A rolling garbage can holds rakes and gardening tools, and can roll out to the garden with you.
- Box lids of all shapes and sizes work wonders as drawer dividers.
- Egg cartons and muffin tins make perfect jewelry organizers inside of drawers.
- A foil cooking tray placed by the entryway can collect muddy and snowy shoes and boots.
- Mugs and weighted glass cups make perfect organizers for pens on a desk; paintbrushes and scissors in the craft room; or even eyeliners, Q-tips, and nail files in the bathroom.
- Decorator icing tips can be used as ring holders.
- A tote bag with a hole cut in the bottom or empty tissue boxes hold plastic shopping bags. There's no need to buy a fancy bag holder.
- Self-adhesive shoe grips, non-skid chair pads, rubber non-slip bath grips or rubber bands can all be placed on the ends of hangers to stop clothing from slipping.
- A towel bar installed on the inside of your kitchen cabinet door works wonders for holding pot lids.
- Putting a ball of yarn or gift-wrapping ribbon in an old funnel makes it easy to dispense without tangles.

- Baby food jars can house screws and nails in a work area. To keep them off the workbench, mount the lids to a beam: the jar can screw into the lid.
- Tuck photographs into a Rolodex file by attaching a photograph to each card, and use it as a countertop photo album.
- A dish rack can store coloring books and other art supplies. Stack the books like plates, between the prongs. Store markers, crayons, and pencils in the utensil caddy.
- A garden hose winder is a perfect tool for winding up strings of holiday lights.
- Place shower caddies in your laundry room, pantry, and garden area. Instead of storing shampoo they can hold spot remover, spices, or seed packets.
- A cardboard six-pack bottle holder makes a perfect picnic or barbecue organizer. Slip napkins, condiments, and silverware into the slots.
- Hang jewelry from a coat rack or hat rack for tangle-free organization.
- Screw doorknobs into the wall and hang things from them, like a dog leash or umbrella.
- Hooks mounted underneath kitchen cabinets can hold everyday coffee mugs.
- Nails hammered into the walls can serve as hook for belts, ties, or other accessories.
- Photo albums can be used to store business cards; simply slide them into the pockets. Smaller travel-size photo albums can fit in your purse or briefcase.
- A magnetic knife organizer can double as a holder for the recipe you're preparing. Other magnetic organizers tucked in convenient places like the front door can hold keys and reminders. You can even place one by your desk and then

stick a magnet on the back of small jars and tins so they stick to the organizer.

- In addition to using binder clips to organize papers, use one to hold the cords hanging from blinds out of sight. Tie up the cord and clip it to the back of the blind.
- A business card holder fits your favorite sweetener and even a tea bag so they don't break open in your purse.
- Film canisters can double as postage stamp dispensers if you cut a slit in the side of the canister and thread through the first stamp in the coil. The canisters also make great coin holders. Keep one in the car for toll money and one at home for Laundromat change. They also store pins, buttons, tacks, and other small items. Be sure to label each canister since they all look the same from the outside.
- The cardboard insert from the center of a toilet tissue roll can be the perfect place to store an extension cord without tangling it. Coil the cord and then slide it through the tube. You can make a note on the tube to remind yourself how long the cord is so you can grab the length you need.
- Nail polish doubles as a way to color-code your keys. Lay your keys on a flat surface and apply a coat or two of a different shade to the top of each key.
- Once you finish all the mints in a tin, keep the tin and use it to store clean tissues. One in your purse, one in your car, and one in your beach bag means you'll always have a clean, dry tissue when you need one.
- A napkin holder holds bills to be paid and incoming mail. It stores mail vertically, eliminating paper piles.
- A three- or five-tiered file rack meant to hold file folders staggered on your desktop can be used in a kitchen cabinet to sort cookie sheets, cutting boards, and muffin tins.

- A wine rack can be put to good use holding rolled magazines or towels.
- Bobby pins double as a bookmark to mark your stopping point.
- Use mismatched socks or a coffee filter as a cleaning rag
- A lint roller cleans lampshades quickly.
- Ice cube trays can be used to organize kids' shell and rock collections.
- A desk organizer can hold makeup.
- Poke a paintbrush through a plastic coffee can lid before painting to catch drips.
- Poke the stick of an ice-cream pop through a muffin paper to stop messy drips.
- Paper from your shredder makes great packing material.
- A spice rack can hold crafting supplies or sewing notions.
- A piece of screen stapled to a picture frame and hung on the wall works as an earring organizer. You also can hook earrings over the edge of a candleholder.
- A tension-mount shower bar can be placed in a closet or other room for extra hanging space.
- Old mailboxes placed next to your garden can store frequently used tools. Or, use one near the children's play area to collect sidewalk chalk, jump ropes, and other small items that are easily lost.

## My bookshelf is out of room. What should I do?

First, consider reintroducing yourself to your local library if you haven't been there lately. Borrowing a book to read instead of buying it is a great way to save space and trees. If you love the book and wanted to read it again, you can always buy it later if you really want to. Many libraries have upgraded to computer systems that allow you to reserve and renew books online to avoid a late penalty. Plus, many people report that they don't put a book aside if they only have a designated time to read it. If you prefer to buy books, then keep a running list of book titles you want. Buy a new one only when you finish the one you're reading. This will eliminate your "to-read" pile. Swapping books is another great alternative. You can swap books online or share them with friends and family. Finally, you can donate some of your books to charity. Here are some charities in need of the used books from your bookshelf:

- Darien Book Aid, www.dba.darien.org
- Book Project, www.internationalbookproject.org
- Global Literacy Project, www.glpinc.org
- Prison Reader, www.prisonreader.org
- Reader to Reader, www.readertoreader.org

You can swap books at the following places:

- PaperBack Swap, www.paperbackswap.com
- BookCrossing, www.bookcrossing.com
- BookMooch, www.bookmooch.com
- TitleTrader, www.titletrader.com
- Swaptree, www.swaptree.com
- SwitchPlanet, www.switchplanet.com

## How can I avoid buying wrapping paper?

Make your own gift wrap. These earth-friendly gift-wrapping ideas help you repurpose items that might otherwise become clutter:

- Use a piece of artwork your child created.
- Adhere crossword puzzles, Sudoku puzzles, crosswords, or find-a-words to plain paper.
- Use an embroidered napkin or decorative scarf tied with a cord.

- Create a tower of gift boxes held together with ribbon.
- Use a glue gun to adhere gemstones to wrapping paper.
- Use a rubber stamp on Kraft paper.
- Use a wrap that coordinates with the gift (e.g., an old map to wrap a history book).
- Wrap multiple gifts together. (e.g., if you're wrapping a CD player and CDs, place the CDs in the player and just wrap the player).
- During the holidays, instead of wrapping gifts hang them from the Christmas tree branches.
- Use an embellishment that coordinates with the gift (e.g., cookie cutters tied on with ribbon for a set of bake ware).
- And to avoid buying traditional to/from tags, use a photo of the recipient to identify whom the gift is for. This is a great way to recycle duplicate photos.

## What can I do with furniture I'd like to use in nontraditional ways?

There are tons of options for using furniture in nontraditional ways. For example, a dresser can serve as a dining room sideboard, a trunk could be your family room coffee table, or a small chest of drawers works well as an end table. You also can make existing furniture more functional. Make a traditional coffee table or end table more functional by slipping a basket, container, or rolling bin beneath it.

## Cases of bottled water take up lots of space in my pantry. Once used, the bottles fill up my recycling bin. Is there a way to organize this clutter?

There's a simple alternative to bottled water: buy a stainless steel thermos and fill it with tap water. If you're not a big fan of your local tap water, add an inexpensive carbon filter to your tap. Take this advice, and you avoid carrying all those heavy bottles of water home, paying for water, and storing all those recyclable bottles. It will save you time, money, and sanity.

## I'd like to organize a recycling center at home. How do I get started?

First, let me share my routine. I have a bin in my kitchen that catches just about all the recycling materials. I don't sort them in the kitchen; they just get dumped in after they are rinsed and flattened. I use a can crusher to save space. You can find one at most home goods or home improvement stores, and it is well worth the minimal investment. When the bin is full, I take it to the garage and sort each item into the appropriate bins. In my office, I have a decorative basket for paper recycling, which includes the shreds from the shredder.

The first step in organizing your own recycling center is finding out what is recycled in your area. Check your town's website or call for recycling information. Ask if items like glass, aluminum, paper, cardboard, and plastic are accepted and whether there are any restrictions, like not mixing colored glass. Find out what the pickup schedule is and how you can dispose of hazardous waste should you ever have any. Mark the recycling pickup days on your calendar, and mark the day before the pickup days as a reminder to take out the recycling.

Based on what materials your town recycles, decide how many containers you'll need. For example, if your town accepts number one and number two plastics but requires them to be separated, you'll need two bins for plastics.

Label each bin clearly so you know what goes where. You also can note which items go in which bin, so you don't always have to search for the recycling number on the item. Just like any new routine, it will take some getting used to. Once recycling is a habit, you won't even have to think about it—it will just happen automatically.

## Is there a better way to organize the tangle of wire hangers from the dry cleaner?

Some home goods stores sell a hanger organizer. It is a triangular piece of wood with three prongs. The hangers slip over the prongs and stay in place. Whenever possible, bring your hangers to the dry cleaners for them to reuse. Many tailor shops accept donations of hangers, or you could donate them to a thrift store.

## How can I remember to take canvas bags to the store?

First, gather all of the tote bags you have at home. The goal is to have enough bags so you can store some in multiple locations. Keep a bunch of canvas bags in your car and a few others by the front door or the door to the garage. After you use the bags for groceries, fold them and place them near the door so you can pick them up on your way out. Some styles of bags fold up into pouches small enough to tuck in your purse. After you've used one of those, simply fold it up and put it back in your purse for your next shopping trip. Once you're accustomed to grabbing the bags before heading into the store, you won't have to give it a second thought.

## How can I organize all of my household cleaners?

A great way to simplify is to choose homemade, chemical-free cleaners that safely clean more than one surface. Here are a few recipes for home cleaners:

### *Gentle all-surface cleaner (countertops, stove range, floors, toilet seat, refrigerator doors and shelves, and much more)*

Mix one cup of white vinegar and one cup cool water in a trigger spray bottle.

For stubborn spots including soap scum and water deposits, warm the solution and douse the area generously; then let stand for ten minutes before cleaning.

### Strong all-surface cleaning solution

Mix one tablespoon of ammonia, 1 tablespoon clear laundry detergent, and two cups cool water in a trigger spray bottle.

### Gentle scouring cleaner (bathtub rings, food residue in refrigerators, kitchen counters, and much more)

Pour baking soda into an empty and clean Parmesan cheese sprinkle-top container or sugar shaker (salt shaker holes are too small).

Sprinkle baking soda onto a damp sponge and go to work.

### Strong scouring paste cleaner (reside around faucets, tub, sink, soap scum, and much more)

Make a paste using one part water and two parts baking soda. Then slather the paste onto tough-to-clean areas, wait ten minutes, and wipe off.

### Toilet bowl cleaner (or hard-to-clean mineral deposits or soap scum)

First, to empty the toilet bowl pour a bucket of water into the bowl so the water is forced out.

Then spray undiluted white vinegar all around the bowl. Scrub with a toilet brush and use a pumice stone (yes, a pumice stone) to remove any stubborn rings.

### Glass and shiny surface spray cleaner (windows, glass, chrome, ceramic tile, and much more)

Mix one cup rubbing (isopropyl) alcohol, one cup cool water, and 1 tablespoon white vinegar in a trigger spray bottle.

### Strong soaking solution (showerheads, faucets with mineral deposits)

Pour a half cup of undiluted white vinegar into a plastic food storage bag. Use a rubber band to attach the bag to the faucet or showerhead. Be sure the item is soaking in the solution. Let stand for two to six hours, then rinse. Use an old toothbrush or old baby bottle washer, if necessary, to clear the holes of any residue.

Clearly label each container so you know its intended use. Also, you can write the recipe directly on the bottle so you can refill it easily.

**Note:** If you're concerned about a vinegar smell left behind, don't be. Once the surface is dry, the aroma disappears.

## How can I use or reuse dryer sheets for organizing and cleaning up?

Here are the top fifteen ways to use a new dryer sheet:

Use a wet dryer sheet (it will foam up) to:

1. Wash or touch up sneakers
2. Clean greasy, grimy hands
3. Dissolve soap scum from shower doors
4. Take black marks off vinyl tiles
5. Clean baked-on food from a cooking pan. Place a sheet in the pan, fill it with water, let it sit overnight, then clean as usual.

Use the sheet dry to:

1. Prevent musty luggage by tucking a sheet inside before storing
2. Collect pet hair by rubbing the area

3. Remove beach sand from your legs by running the sheet gently over your legs
4. Eliminate static electricity from blinds; wipe the blinds with a sheet to prevent dust from resettling
5. Deodorize things like shoes or sneakers; tuck a sheet inside overnight or in the bottom of garbage cans to eliminate odors
6. Eliminate static electricity from your television or computer screens by dusting with the sheet
7. Freshen the air in your car by tossing a sheet under the front seat or tucking it in one of the air vents
8. Keep bugs away; tuck one in your belt waistband or in the back of your collar so it sticks out
9. Pick up dust bunnies and cobwebs; wipe in corners of rooms
10. Remove deodorant marks from clothes

## What's the best way to recycle items such as cell phones and batteries?

Log on to www.Earth911.org for information about how to recycle harmful items. You can also check out:

- www.LooseFillPackaging.com, for places to get rid of your packing material
- www.RedJellyFish.org, for places to donate your old cell phones
- www.RecycledGoods.com, for places to donate your old computer

# Chapter 13

# REAL MOMENTS— SPECIFIC ORGANIZING QUESTIONS

- I scooped up piles of clutter when guests were coming, and now I have bags and boxes of clutter that I need to look through. There may be important items in them, so I can't simply toss everything. What can I do?

- My husband drops his junk on my clean kitchen counter. What can I do?

- Is it bad to have duplicates in my home? I have three pairs of scissors, five pairs of reading glasses, and other duplicates.

- My spouse leaves paper piles in the office and junk piles on countertops. We have frequent disagreements about this, and it's putting a strain on our marriage. What can we do?

- How can I get someone to pick up his or her belongings that were left with me for storage?

- I finally get a space organized, and before long it's back to being messy. What am I doing wrong?

- If my home doesn't have a mudroom, will it be harder to stay organized?

- I switch purses often to coordinate with my outfit, but I waste time dumping out the contents of one purse to fill another. What do you suggest to save time?

- I have a bunch of half-full purses stashed in my closet. When I switch to a new purse, I never fully clean out the old one. Do you have any suggestions?

- I had an emergency pipe leak and needed to pull everything out of the room so the plumber could work. Now I have a huge mess and no idea where to start. Any ideas?

- I have to have an electrician in to rewire our main box but I can't make the appointment until I clean out the space so he can work. What can I do?

- My family and friends keep giving me stuff they don't want, and I don't want it either. How can I get them to stop?

## I scooped up piles of clutter when guests were coming, and now I have bags and boxes of clutter that I need to look through. There may be important items in them, so I can't simply toss everything. What can I do?

Start by committing to stop scooping up piles of clutter this way. Knowing that you won't continue to add more to the backlog will lift a weight off your shoulders. To get out of the habit, try to put things away as soon as you are finished using them. Every evening do a quick house tour and pick up anything that is out of place. If guests are expected and you have items that need to be picked up, go ahead and collect them but don't hide them away—remember, out of sight, out of mind. Instead put them somewhere like the top of your bed. That hopefully will force you to put them away that evening. Then check your calendar and block off increments of time when you can work on the backlog. Do not focus on all of the clutter at once; your goal is to sort one handful from one bag, then another handful, and so on. It might seem like clearing the backlog will take a lifetime, but if you break up the task and continually take action it will go a lot faster than you can imagine. Try bringing a small amount of items to the kitchen to sort as your children do their homework, or to the living room to work on while you watch a show. Your choices for the items you find are keep, toss/recycle/shred, give away, or not sure. You can set up four boxes with these labels and place items into each box. Then deal with each box at the end of each sorting session. Otherwise, the boxes themselves will become backlog.

## My husband drops his junk on my clean kitchen counter. What can I do?

First, take a deep breath. Most likely he's not doing it to make you crazy; he simply has a bad habit. The good news is that this is easily corrected. Choose a spot near where he enters the kitchen and place a single basket there. Or pick a new spot in the kitchen for his stuff, such as a spare kitchen drawer. Then show him the new spot and ask him if he thinks it will work. (If he's not in agreement it will never work.) Once you've agreed on the new location for his junk, try it out for a week or two and see if you need to make any changes. To break the old routine, you might have to leave a bold reminder note on the counter. Finally, remember to tell your husband how appreciative you are when he gets it right, and try to bite your tongue and just move the stuff if he forgets. If you focus on the times he gets it right, he'll be more likely to get it right more often.

## Is it bad to have duplicates in my home? I have three pairs of scissors, five pairs of reading glasses, and other duplicates.

That depends. Sometimes having duplicates makes life easier and saves time, like having a pair of scissors in almost every room of the house. Other times having duplicates means you take less care of the items, because you know you have others if you lose the original. Having multiple pairs of reading glasses might make it difficult to find a pair when you need one, because they can be anywhere in the house. A better plan might be to designate one place for a single pair of glasses and always put them back when you are done. If you already own duplicates, instead of giving them away place them in a box, clearly label it, and put it away. That way, when you need that particular item you have it on hand but out of the way.

## My spouse leaves paper piles in the office and junk piles on countertops. We have frequent disagreements about this, and it's putting a strain on our marriage. What can we do?

It's true that opposites tend to attract, and that includes opposite organizing styles. Try designating common areas of the home as "no clutter zones," so that each person feels comfortable in those rooms. To keep the areas clutter-free, allocate a spot within those areas for stuff to be placed. For example, in a living room an ottoman with a lift-off lid might be the spot for newspapers and catalogs instead of piling them next to the couch. In addition to "no clutter zones," both of you should have a place where you can do what you want, without comment or criticism from the other. For example, one person might get the back corner of the garage or a small closet to collect whatever he or she likes, as long as it does not creep past a certain point.

## How can I get someone to pick up his or her belongings that were left with me for storage?

A deadline is really the only solution that works. The person storing belongings at your home knows the items are safe, and unless you are charging him or her rent, the storage space is free. That person has no motivation to pick up the items. A deadline from you will be just the motivation he or she needs. It might not be easy to tell someone that you need to evict his or her belongings, but usually the news is met with understanding and thankfulness for having been so patient. Set a deadline that works for both of you, be very clear about what is expected, and stick to it. Extending the deadline will only show that you're not serious.

Another option is to invite the owners of the items over for a day of packing, especially if they are family members such as children who are starting their own lives. Everyone should bring boxes, and you can all reminisce as you pack up the treasures. If you are the one who is holding on to your children's unwanted items under the guise that your grandchildren might want them one day, consider that safety standards for toys and baby items have changed over the years. The items in storage, like your children's old toys, probably are not clean enough or safe enough to pass along. Take a photo of the items and toss them. You'll still have the memories, and now you'll have the space.

## I finally get a space organized, and before long it's back to being messy. What am I doing wrong?

It sounds like you might be under the impression that once a space is organized, it will stay that way. That generally is not the case. Although you might intend to always put things back when you're finished using them, it isn't always possible. You might be busy, you might forget, or something else might prevent you from keeping an area tidy. However, a quick daily or weekly run through an area will help keep it organized.

## If my home doesn't have a mudroom, will it be harder to stay organized?

No. In fact, many people who live in homes with mudrooms often wish they didn't have one to clean and organize. While a mudroom is a great transition space, you can create a space that will function the same way. You'll need hooks for jackets, a place for backpacks or other bags, and a spot for outgoing items like mail. If you have a closet near the door you use most often, that can act as a makeshift mudroom. Simply relocate the closet's contents.(Yes, you'll have to store it elsewhere, but the benefit is worth it.) Install hooks on one side wall of the closet for jackets. On the back of the closet door hang a sixteen-pocket clear plastic shoe holder. This is where you'll store mail, sunglasses, keys, mittens, and much more. Inside the closet, place a clearly labeled basket for each family member to hold shoes, bags, or backpacks. If there is a top shelf in the closet, use it to store out-of-season accessories. If there is no closet near the door you use most often, you can opt for an armoire or a floor-to-ceiling bookshelf placed as near to the door as possible.

### I switch purses often to coordinate with my outfit, but I waste time dumping out the contents of one purse to fill another. What do you suggest to save time?

Having duplicates of some of the most common purse items can be helpful. It might make sense to have doubles or even triples of things like your everyday lip gloss and a small mirror so you'll always have them in the purse you are using. Group like items together and store them in small bags like makeup bags or clear ziplock bags (a great idea since you easily can see what's inside). One bag might hold makeup, another might hold a pen and notepaper, and yet another might hold coupons and store discount key tags. Grouping items this way will help you take along only what you need. For example, when you're going shopping you might grab all the bags; when you're heading out to dinner you can leave behind the bag that holds the coupons.

### I have a bunch of half-full purses stashed in my closet. When I switch to a new purse, I never fully clean out the old one. Do you have any suggestions?

First, stop switching to a new purse without cleaning out the old one. When you do switch purses, take an extra moment to dump the old purse out at the same time. Although I'd prefer you dump out the contents and immediately sort them, if you can't, at least dump out the contents. That way, you can rest assured that the next item you pull out of your purse will be clean and ready to use. Put the clean bag away, and when you have time, sort the odds and ends you spilled out. Many times the leftovers just need to be tossed, so go ahead and replace what's left of the eyeliner pencil you think is still worth saving or the trial-size hand cream you picked up two years ago. You might be surprised to learn about all the icky things I've seen left in purses over the years: things like turkey sandwiches (or at least that's what we thought it was when my client found it almost a year later); an orange that was anything but orange by the time we located it; a bottle of perfume that had slowly leaked, ruining a very expensive evening bag; a tax return check with four zeros in it; and a driver's license that had since been replaced. Dump out all the pockets of your purse before filling up a new one to avoid these and other nasty consequences.

## I had an emergency pipe leak and needed to pull everything out of the room so the plumber could work. Now I have a huge mess and no idea where to start. Any ideas?

It is understandable that in the emergency things needed to be moved quickly and probably got tossed and jumbled together. Rather than a problem, I look at this as an opportunity to put back what you want to keep in an organized way. You would have had to take it all out to organize it anyway, so think of this as an unexpected project. Chances are it feels overwhelming because it is a big pile, but that's all right—you're going to start small. Instead of working on everything at once, simply work in sections. If it makes it easier, take a laundry basket full of miscellaneous stuff into another room to sort it. Otherwise, you can just divide the items in your mind and work on a section at a time. The most important thing to remember is that your goal is to work for a specific amount of time on the project, not to finish it. If your goal is to finish, you may lose motivation before you are done, whereas if your goal is to work for twenty minutes a day, then each and every day you have a chance to succeed at your goal! Remember brownie organizing!

## I have to have an electrician in to rewire our main box but I can't make the appointment until I clean out the space so he can work. What can I do?

You'll want to get to this as soon as possible, *before* it becomes an emergency, whatever the situation is. It may be electrical, a furnace, your cable, or anything you'd likely hire a professional to take care of. This may sound a little scary, but I'd make the appointment. Not for tomorrow, of course, but for sometime soon, maybe six to eight weeks from now. Once you have the appointment, you have a deadline to motivate you, and you can work backward, figuring out how much time you need to set aside each week to get the project done. Let's say you need to clear out half a basement, keeping in mind that it does *not* have to be perfect. You'd want to set aside about fifteen hours. Chances are you don't have a fifteen-hour block of space in your calendar, and even if you did, you might not have the stamina to work for fifteen hours straight. So divide the time over the next few weeks on your calendar. Remember to be realistic, one hour a day for fifteen straight days will most likely not happen. It might look good on paper, but you'll want a break. Some days you'll just be too busy, and that's okay. You need to plan around anything already on your calendar that may take up time—holidays or other special events, like a town-wide clean-up day where you could put out items you may find while you are organizing. Maybe you'll do a two-hour block first thing on a Saturday to get the ball rolling, and follow it up with one to two hours a few days a week. To keep yourself on track, try to schedule your sessions around a routine you already have in place. For example, if you have a favorite TV show on Wednesday nights, you might tell yourself you'll bring a pile of stuff to sort in front of the television, or you'll watch your show after you put in an hour of organizing time. Before you know it, the space will be clear, you'll have met your deadline, and you can move forward with your appointment. Remember—it doesn't have to be perfect, it just has to be done.

## My family and friends keep giving me stuff they don't want, and I don't want it either. How can I get them to stop?

This is a little tricky, because you don't want to come across as ungrateful. However, if you don't refuse these gifts, your home will be overrun with hand-me-downs you can't use. Depending on how close you are to the person and how understanding he or she is, try being straightforward and simply say thanks but no thanks. You also could say that you have too much stuff of your own, and you don't want to accept more things that might go to waste. Most likely people are giving you their stuff because they're not aware of an alternative. In that case, give them the names of a few local charities that would be thankful for the donations. As a last resort, you can explain that you're reading a book about getting organized, and the book's author says before you can accept more things from others you have to get your own stuff under control. So, until further notice, you're banned from accepting more things.

Dear Reader,

Now that I've answered your questions, I have two questions for you: What one small step are you going to take to regain control of your life, and when are you going to take it? Today can be your day—the day you take back your life. It's not nearly as difficult as you might imagine; it all starts with one small step. Getting started is usually the hardest part, but once you start everything will fall into place.

I truly hope I've answered your questions about getting organized. I enjoy nothing more than when readers share their success stories with me. I hope you will send yours along; I'd love to hear all about what you've done. Please contact me toll free at 1-866-294-9900 or through my website, www.JamieNovak.com. Finally, I'm sure you can tell that I made every attempt to cover the most frequently asked questions and to offer earth-friendly ideas. However, I can't think of everything, so if you have a question I didn't answer or a suggestion I didn't mention, I'd love to know about it. Tell me what it is, and I just may use it in an upcoming book.

Wishing you a life you love,
Jamie

P.S. I'd be honored if you invite me to be a part of your next get-together. No matter where you live, if you and a few friends are getting together to discuss the book, I can join you by speakerphone. If you're a member of an organization that has an annual conference, I'd love to give the keynote address or lead a workshop. Simply contact my office so we can compare calendars.

Would you like to meet with other people who are looking to create a life they love by living life one bite at a time? I invite you to create a Bite-Size Organizing discussion group. It's so easy; just use this book as your guide.

## Ten Simple Steps to Creating Your Bite-Size Organizing Discussion Group

1. Locate at least one other person who struggles with getting everything done. (Consider your children's classmates' mothers, coworkers, friends, family, neighbors, friends or acquaintances from your house of worship, and other parents from your children's day care or extracurricular activities.)
2. Invite the person or people to the group.
3. Choose a place to meet. You might opt to rotate homes or meet in a café or library.
4. Pick a date and time to meet.
5. Decide how often the group will meet—weekly or monthly.
6. Be sure everyone reads chapter 1 of *The Get Organized Answer Book* before your first meeting.
7. Consider designating one person per meeting as a timekeeper to ensure that everyone has a chance to participate.
8. By the end of the meeting, be sure each person has stated a goal he or she plans to accomplish before the next meeting.
9. Assign the next chapter to be read before the next meeting.
10. Stay in touch between meetings to give each other support. Also consider getting free online support through www. JamieNovak.com.

# BITE-SIZE ORGANIZING GROUPS

If you're a professional organizer, coach, therapist, author, trainer, consultant, speaker, or other person looking to meet with other people who want to create a community of people looking to create a life they love by clearing their clutter, then facilitating a Bite-Size Organizing Group might be right for you. No previous experience is necessary, and you don't have to feel comfortable with public speaking. The Bite-Size Organizing Group is a fantastic, fully customizable way to connect with potential clients while creating a supportive community. If you'd like to offer such a program but don't want to start from scratch, consider using the Bite-Size Organizing Group template (provided when you contact my office) as your club resource. Looking for a Bite-Size Organizing Group to join? They're free and open to the public. Most groups meet monthly (some in person and some over the phone) and are great for getting ideas, tips, and motivation! Check out www.JamieNovak.com or call 1-866-294-9900 to locate a Bite-Size Organizing Group near you or to get more information.

# Index

# *About the Author*

**Jamie Novak** is the World's Most Relatable Organizer™ and the first and only authority on Bite-Size Organizing™, although she'd be the first to admit that there are days when even she can't find her left shoe. With almost twenty years of professional organizing and time management coaching behind her, Jamie knows one thing for sure: just because we know what we need to do, that doesn't guarantee we're doing it. So she's taken a unique approach, blending her doable, no-nonsense techniques for organizing and managing time with her "you can do it" attitude, resulting in bite-size ideas that work for how we really live. These are powerful and budget-friendly ideas that anyone can use.

Jamie is a live on-air guest for a line of organizing products with QVC. She's partnered with some of the giants in the home organization industry, including Brother P-Touch and Collectify Home Inventory. She's the organizing expert on NBC's iVillage, and she hosts her own weekly radio show, *Bite-Size Organizing with Jamie*. She's also been a featured organizer on HGTV's *Mission: Organization*. With three books already on bookshelves around the world, Jamie's advice has transformed many lives. She is the go-to expert for the media and has been quoted in countless national magazines. She is also the founder of Bite-Size Organizing Groups, which are free, nationwide discussion groups usually run by professional organizers. You can visit www.JamieNovak.com to find a group near you.

In her own unique and nonjudgmental way, Jamie has been helping busy people clear the clutter, live a life they can enjoy in a home they love, and reach their goals with a clearer head. Her approach is both easy and motivating; she is a natural, and her passion for organizing shines through. Jamie promises not to try to reinvent you. Instead, she helps you find your style and work with it. Her goal is to share real ideas that really work!

Jamie's main office is in Scotch Plains, NJ, where she grew up and still lives. She has a second office in Los Angeles, CA, where she spends a portion of the year. If you'd like to share a success story or submit your favorite tip, view free resources, get an answer to your biggest clutter challenge, register to join Jamie for one of her free classes by phone, or view current contests, visit www.JamieNovak.com.

You can't do it all, and you certainly can't do it all at once—that's why Jamie challenges you to live a life you love one bite at a time!